Poets Re-Imagine Canada

A Primer for a Land beyond Acknowledgements

by the Edmonton Stroll of Poets Society

Gary Garrison, Editor

ISBN
978-1-988777-08-5 (all paper softback)
978-1-988777-08-10-8 (ebook)

Editor: Gary Garrison
Cover Design: Janis Dow Durnin
Cover Photo: Kathy Penner

Printed in Canada by PageMaster Publication Services Inc.

Published by The Stroll of Poets Society
11759 Groat Road, Edmonton, Alberta, T5M 3K6
www.strollofpoets.com
Incorporated as an Alberta non-profit society in 1991.

With sincere gratitude to our sponsors:

Table of Contents

Foreword

Partnering to Build a Better Future: *Aaron Paquette* 1

Preface

Truth Comes before Reconciliation 6

Introduction

Learn. Acknowledge. Celebrate. Re-Imagine. Re-Create. 9

Contributions

Upon Whose Land Do You Stand? *Stefani Alzati* 20
Re-Imagining Our Connections: *Hank Binnema* 22
A Homesteader's Land Acknowledgement:
Audrey Brooks 24
The Secret Pre-History of Cobalt, Ontario: *David Brydges* .26
Names: *Kayleigh Cline* 27
Marking the Boundaries: *Leslie Dawson*............................29
On Being So Ignorant: *Leslie Dawson* 31
The First Poets Here Were Indigenous: *Leslie Dawson*.......33
Mvskoke Motherland: *Dr. Deidra Suwanee Dees* 34
The Land You Live On: *Dr. Deidra Suwanee Dees* 36
Prairie Connections: *Janis Dow Durnin*.............................38
First Nation Footsteps: *Janis Dow Durnin* 39
Gratitude First: *Janis Dow Durnin*.....................................40
Terrible Truths: *Janis Dow Durnin*....................................41
Stride for Stride: *Douglas Elves*...43
This Land: *Lynn Gale*..44
Genocide: Never Again: *Gary Garrison* 45
Resurrection: *Gary Garrison* 47
Buried Truths: *Gary Garrison* 49
Speaking the names: *Trudy Grienauer*...............................51
Learn What Happened, Reflect, Do Something:
Trudy Grienauer...52
This Sacred Land: *Lois Mary Hammond*............................53
A lifetime's journey: *Trevor Hughes* 55

Truth and Reconciliation: *Melle Huizinga* 57
Land Acknowledgement: *Dan Knauss* 59
As I set roots down into this earth: *Josephine LoRe* 61
Shared Treasures: *Dorothy Lowrie* 62
The continuing conversation: *Alice Major* 64
What Land Acknowledgements Mean to Me:
Lavona McIlwraith 65
Not Just a Land Acknowledgement: *Naomi McIlwraith* 68
My Humble Land Acknowledgement to All Stewards
of Treaty 6: *Naomi McIlwraith* 71
The words have been all around: *Don Perkins* 73
When Crow Stole White Noise: *Daniel Poitras* 75
A Gradual Awakening: *Shirley Serviss* 78
The Ground Remembers: A Treaty 6 Territory
Acknowledgement: *patti sinclair* 80
Healing and Hope: *Laurel Sproule* 82
Thank You for Honouring the Earth: *Max Vandersteen* 84

Contributor Biographies 85

Thank You 94

Editor's Notes
Style Decisions Regarding Indigenous Words 96
A Caveat on Terminology 98

Suggestions for Further Reading 101

Internet Resources 103

Indigenous Words for Buffalo/Bison 105

Foreword

Partnering to Build a Better Future

Aaron Paquette

When Naomi McIlwraith asked me to write something to add an Indigenous person's perspective to this book by the Stroll of Poets Society, I was delighted to oblige. I, too, am frustrated that rote, impersonal land acknowledgements have become the norm when what Canada needs is courageous thinking and concrete, personal actions to heal the long-broken relationship between settlers and Indigenous peoples. This book is a welcome step in that direction.

To acknowledge treaty is to acknowledge a responsibility to each other, to acknowledge the obligations that we have to each other that weren't always fulfilled, and to reaffirm that we are willing to do better for this generation and generations to come. When we make treaty or land acknowledgments before meetings, events, legislative sessions, or public engagements, it shows that we recognize that we are neighbours and that we understand the history behind our relationships. Even deeper, that we understand the principles of kinship, of wâhkôhtowin, between all things. This is a practical and responsible way to look at each other, upon whom we depend for survival, and at the world in which we live.

Some politicians have policy and economic reasons to shy away from land acknowledgments. They worry that treaties between Indigenous peoples and the Crown included the promise that Indigenous health and prosperity would be safeguarded through partnership. Indigenous peoples of the past gave up vast amounts of resource wealth for this partnership. That was why they signed the treaties in the first place: to ensure their generations would be equal and well cared for in the lands of their people and allowed the freedom to live their lives. Of course, that didn't happen. So, if you are a politician or a resource-dependent corporation or entity, why would you want to acknowledge a treaty you're not fulfilling? For politicians and others with power or authority, land acknowledgments can show an understanding of Canada's history and communicate to Indigenous peoples a desire for better relationships.

When we acknowledge treaty rights in one province, we are effectively acknowledging all treaties in Canada. This can be further complicated for some when we also introduce the emerging realities of the United Nations Declaration on the Rights of Indigenous Peoples (UNDRIP) in 2007, and the 2023 repudiation by the Vatican of the Doctrine of Discovery.

Either individuals and institutions are going to pass trauma from generation to generation or they're going to pass healing. Part of healing is acknowledgement. That's a simple fact. Through speaking, we begin to weave together our lives, our histories, and our knowledge. We become stronger in the weft and warp, relying on one another and creating new patterns of thought and action. This is vital for our nations, and for all our children—Indigenous, Inuit, Métis, newcomer, settler, and all who live here—to grow in strength and promise. Treaty is that promise. It is up to all of us to fulfill it together.

The following is an example of a treaty acknowledgement I gave in my role as an Edmonton City Councillor.

May 21, 2019 Urban Planning Committee opening remarks

On occasion, council or committee will offer a treaty acknowledgment to begin the proceedings. This is in response to the 94 recommendations made by the Truth and Reconciliation Commission. To many, it can come across as rote, as a signal of virtue, or simply checking off a box. The words become almost a ritual that can be anticipated and spoken but perhaps not always really heard or understood.

So today I would like to offer something a little different. I would like to give, in a brief and small way, an explanation of why we offer treaty acknowledgements and what it actually means to me, and for all of us.

Considering that we are on the tail end of Victoria Day, it seems appropriate to talk about these agreements made with Canada (the British Empire) on behalf of Her Majesty the Queen.

To begin, the numbered treaties in Canada were signed over a period of decades across much of this nation. Indeed, they can be considered the founding documents of this country. They are legal apparatuses that allow Canada as we know it to exist. The treaties were signed not in culmination of war but as a formation and certainty of peace.

Treaty 6 was agreed to by two different peoples with two very different world views. Municipalities, provinces, and the federal government are bound by the language of laws. The English language is a noun-based language that, by its nature, lends itself to the concept of physical, time-based ownership. The Cree language is a verb-based language that, while it certainly has nouns, is more focused on action, relationships, and an understanding of cycles and impermanence. As you can imagine, this led to two entirely different understandings of what treaty words conveyed.

This difference could have led us to fundamentally important understandings of one another and concepts that could grow and strengthen relationship, and in many ways, one could argue it did. However, it also led to some of the most terrible actions we can imagine. It led to acts that produced many of the social ills we see today when we think of Canada and First Nations,

Métis, and Inuit people. This was, in large part, due to the Indian Act: a rarity in that it is a solely race-based piece of legislation and a fundamental tool by which treaties were weakened.

The following are some of the impacts of the Indian Act, and it is by no means a comprehensive list. The Indian Act:

- denied women status
- introduced residential schools
- created reserves
- renamed individuals with European names
- restricted First Nations from leaving the reserve without permission from an Indian Agent (the pass system was a policy endorsed by the government; it was never an Order in Council or regulation but was by nature designed to keep First Nations on the reserve)
- physically relocated reserves away from municipalities if it was deemed expedient
- denied First Nations people the right to vote
- forbade First Nations from forming political organizations
- forbade First Nations from speaking their native language
- forbade First Nations from practicing their traditional religion
- forbade western First Nations from appearing in any public dance, show, exhibition, stampede or pageant wearing traditional regalia
- declared potlatch, sundance, and all other cultural ceremonies illegal.

The Indian Act imposed great personal, economic, and cultural tragedy on First Nations. This legacy continues to affect many communities, families and individuals today.

These acts of genocide did not just occur in the past. Their echoes persist. More than half of the children in care in Canada are Indigenous. First Nations, Métis, and Inuit women and girls continue to go missing in a country where they represent a small percentage of the overall population but a disproportionately large percentage of crimes are committed against them. The majority of ills are a direct result of generations of abuse, neglect, and dishonouring of treaty agreements at the hands of the federal government.

Many people feel resentful when they hear these sobering statistics and more. They should not. No one here is to blame. But Canada has been the beneficiary of this colonialism, and treaty acknowledgments are one way by which we begin to heal this relationship so we might prosper together. Our yesterdays have been determined; our tomorrows are waiting for us to decide.

I will add at this point that everything that happened was technically legal. The law can control a person's autonomy. It can control their body, their right to express themselves, and their freedom to live and love as they feel they should.

As I give this acknowledgement, I ask you to reflect on the power and purpose of government and to ponder your place within it.

Treaty Acknowledgement: I'll call the meeting to order, and acknowledge that council meets on the traditional land of Treaty 6 territory. And I'll also acknowledge the diverse Indigenous peoples whose ancestors' footsteps have marked this territory for centuries, such as: Cree, Dene, Saulteaux, Blackfoot, Nakota Sioux, as well as Métis and Inuit, and now settlers from around the world.

Preface

Truth Comes before Reconciliation

By opening this book, you are already part of a solution. A problem is those impersonal Indigenous land acknowledgements we all hear at the beginning of far too many public events in Canada these days. A *New Yorker* article notes that "they sound like microwave warranties,"[1] not the step toward reconciliation they are supposed to be. These boilerplate statements are sometimes even pre-recorded and replayed over a sound system in a disembodied monotone. Although they may be better than nothing, the very process reeks of insincerity. The intentions may be good, but we wonder if people who do acknowledgements this way are so comfortable in the Canada they know that they don't realize a better Canada is just over the horizon, if they would only risk a step in that direction.

The Edmonton Stroll of Poets Society created this book to challenge ourselves and others to get personal about the work of reconciliation. The book goes beyond lip service and develops new ways of speaking, new ways of thinking, new ways of acting, new ways of connecting with others to make the Canada of the future a place where racism is behind us and justice is all around us.

Canadians have a reputation for being quick to say, "Sorry," but all too often in our relationships with Indigenous peoples that's all we do, as if that word has the power to erase five centuries of racial injustice. Yet too many of us tacitly support governments who have enforced and perpetuated the injustices of the Indian Act and its various iterations since it was first passed in 1876. In his Foreword, Aaron Paquette lists ways the Act continues to

---

[1] Stephen Marche, "Canada's Impossible Acknowledgment," *The New Yorker*, September 7, 2017.

mistreat Indigenous peoples in Canada in our name, using our tax dollars.

The poets in this book do what poets do. We start with our personal experiences and stretch our perceptions of the wider world to include uncomfortable social and historical facts. We imagine a better Canada and suggest how to get there. Being writers, our medium is words. Those words come from our hearts and reveal how we have pushed our thinking into uncharted territory. We present ourselves as mentors for readers like you to follow our example and do something similar yourself.

Be aware that the task involves personal risk. All too often we find comfort in national myths of freedom, equality, democracy, and the rule of law, of Canada as a force for peace and justice around the world. All of these myths are only partly true. In fact, we, the members of the committee who created this book, think it's better to consider these as goals to work toward rather than accomplishments and reasons for self-congratulation. To do this right, we all need to open ourselves up to disturbing facts about things like unmarked graves of Indigenous children at residential schools, the over-representation of Indigenous peoples in the child welfare and prison systems, and the disproportionate number of missing and murdered Indigenous women and girls.

Truths like these are ugly and painful to acknowledge. But consider the reality for young adult Germans today, 80 years after World War II ended. They live in a country where even to fly the swastika Nazi flag or wear the symbol is a criminal offence. The centre of Berlin features a 19,000 square meter Holocaust Memorial consisting of 2,711 grave-like stones visitors can walk through, as in a cemetery, to help them grasp the immensity of the Nazis' crime against the Jews: six million murdered. These young adults did not participate in the genocide, but their grandparents and great-grandparents did. In her book *Caste*, Isabel Wilkerson tells of some young Germans who took a guided tour of the memorial. The guide asks them, "Do you as Germans feel any guilt for what the Germans did?" They answer, "We were not here. We ourselves did not do this. But we do feel that, as the younger generation, we should acknowledge and accept the responsibility. And for the generations that come after us, we should be the guardians of the truth."[2]

We must find steps, concrete actions each of us can take to make a better future for all of us, Indigenous and settler alike. We must begin by committing ourselves to be "guardians of the truth," no matter how difficult and no matter if that truth is 500 years old or still happening right now.

Words can help us process new knowledge and experience. Words are not enough, but to speak them sincerely and knowledgeably is a concrete act, the beginning of the necessary journey toward a fairer Canada for all of us. This book provides suggestions and resources for you to get more deeply involved.

Land Acknowledgments Project Committee
Leslie Y. Dawson, Janis Dow Durnin, Gary Garrison,
Naomi McIlwraith

---

[2] Isabel Wilkerson, *Caste: The Origin of Our Discontents* (New York: Penguin Random House, 2023), 349.

Introduction

Learn. Acknowledge. Celebrate. Re-Imagine. Re-Create.

"Canada must move from apology to action,"[3] said Justice Murray Sinclair, the Ojibwe man who chaired the Truth and Reconciliation Commission of Canada (TRC), upon release of the commission's final report in 2015. That report contained 94 very specific calls to action.[4] For most Canadians, the most obvious action taken during the last nine years has been the practice of acknowledging, at the start of public events, that those events take place on Indigenous land and that both settlers and Indigenous people are "treaty people." But the TRC did not include so-called land acknowledgements among its 94 calls to action.

Prime Minister Justin Trudeau made one of the first noteworthy land acknowledgements in 2016 in an address to the Assembly of First Nations: "Before I begin, I'd like to recognize the Algonquin Nation, on whose traditional territory we are gathering. We acknowledge them as the past, present and future caretakers of this land."[5] Since then, land acknowledgements have routinely appeared on websites, email signatures, social media biographies, as well as at the beginning of public events and elsewhere.

When the National Inquiry into Missing and Murdered Indigenous Women and Girls (MMIWG) issued its final report

---

[3] https://www.thecanadianencyclopedia.ca/en/article/truth-and-reconciliation-commission, Ry Morand, "Truth and Reconciliation Commission," September 24, 2015, last edited October 5, 2020.

[4] For text of the entire report, see https://nctr.ca/, the website of the National Centre for Truth and Reconciliation.

[5] Lynn Gehl, "Land Acknowledgement," March 22, 2022, last edited May 6, 2022, https://www.thecanadianencyclopedia.ca/en/article/land-acknowledgment

in 2019, it made 231 recommendations. Recommendation 15.2 was to "Decolonize by learning the true history of Canada and Indigenous history in your local area. Learn about and celebrate Indigenous Peoples' history, cultures, pride, and diversity, acknowledging the land you live on and its importance to local Indigenous communities, both historically and today."[6]

Learn. Acknowledge. Celebrate. These three acts of reconciliation are at the heart of this book, not as ends in themselves but as means to encourage further concrete actions: imagining a better Canada, supporting Indigenous businesses, cultivating friendships with individual Indigenous people, connecting with Indigenous organizations, and working to change socio-political-cultural-legal systems that embody biased history and racial injustice. The first step, though, is to learn, and the first part to learn is the history. Without a more complete understanding of our national and local history, land acknowledgements are guaranteed to be mere lip service.

What does it mean to say that Indigenous and non-Indigenous people alike are "treaty people"? A treaty is typically a formal agreement between independent, sovereign nations. Before the British Royal Proclamation of 1763, treaties with Indigenous peoples in North America were primarily for mutual defence and trade. Starting in the early 1600s, such treaties between Indigenous nations and Dutch, French, and English colonial governments did not focus on land ownership, even though acquiring Indigenous land for settlement was in the minds of individual settlers, if not officially at the negotiating table. The Royal Proclamation of 1763 confirmed that Indigenous nations were sovereign over their own territories, and it was the

---

[6] https://www.mmiwg-ffada.ca/final-report/
It's worth noting that the word "acknowledgement" includes the word "knowledge." As one etymology website explains in simple language, "'knowledge' is what you know, *acknowledging* is showing that you know." https://www.vocabulary.com/dictionary/acknowledge

foundation for nation-to-nation treaty-making in the many decades after it.

We have to ask ourselves, "How fair could these negotiations ever be, considering not only the language barriers but the profound clash of cultures and the imbalance of power?" Europeans brought with them their Judeo-Christian god and a mandate to convert non-Christians to abandon their gods and become Christian.[7] Christian churches taught that the Earth itself is something to master and control.[8] Indigenous peoples had a variety of creation stories and spiritual practices, but they all saw themselves as collaborators with and part of nature. They had a deep dedication to and knowledge of their land and honoured the animals, the wind, the rain, the sun, the air, and the soil as well as other humans as members of their family. On the other hand, Europeans had steel and guns, but even before armed invasions or treaty negotiations began, European diseases such as cholera and smallpox killed 90 percent of Indigenous peoples in the Americas and devastated their social order.

In addition, according to the *Canadian Encyclopedia*, "rather than sacred pacts between independent nations," treaties were, to Europeans, "real estate deals by which the Crown purchased Indigenous lands and provided them with reserves and one-time

---

[7] In the Gospel of Mark, Jesus commissions his disciples to "teach all nations, baptizing them in the name of the Father, and of the Son, and of the Holy Ghost." Mark 16:19, King James Version. These words, like all Bible verses in English, are translated from other languages and interpreted to mean a variety of things. Scholars and church leaders have argued for centuries over what Jesus actually said and have interpreted them many different ways.

[8] The Judeo-Christian creation story says God created man to rule the Earth: "And God said, Let us make man in our image, after our likeness: and let them have dominion over the fish of the sea, and over the fowl of the air, and over the cattle, and over all the earth, and over every creeping thing that creepeth upon the earth." Genesis 1:26, King James Version.

or continual payments in return."[9] Those payments were and remain a pittance compared to the value of the land, and the Crown typically broke its other treaty promises and treated Indigenous peoples horribly. In fact, Indigenous people who signed treaty agreements usually signed under duress. A noteworthy example was Chief Big Bear, who signed Treaty 6 in 1882 only after his people were driven to the brink of death by starvation. Furthermore, evidence indicates that many government representatives never intended to live up to their side of these agreements.[10] On the other side, Indigenous peoples understood that the treaties confirmed their rights of self-government and were agreements to allow settlers onto land they would all share, not land the government would simply take while it forced its native peoples onto reserves.

When Canadians refer to "unceded land," they imply that other land was, in fact, ceded. But no Indigenous land was ever given up. From the Indigenous perspective, land ownership was an impossibility: nobody could ever own land. Aimée Craft presents convincing evidence that "the concepts of surrender and extinguishment of title were never raised or discussed at the negotiations" for Treaty 1. She says that if the surrender of land had been discussed, it would have precipitated "an immediate breakdown in the negotiations."[11] Many scholars have concluded, based on a variety of documents, eyewitness sources,

---

[9] Gretchen Albers, updated by, "Treaties with Indigenous Peoples in Canada," last edited September 11,2017, https://www.thecanadianencyclopedia.ca/en/article/aboriginal-treaties

[10] The report of Canada's Truth and Reconciliation Commission quotes U.S. General William Tecumseh Sherman, a military leader in the U.S. Civil War and Commander General during the Indian wars from 1869-83. Sherman said, "We have made more than one thousand treaties with various Indian tribes, and have not kept one of them." https://ehprnh2mwo3.exactdn.com/wp-content/uploads/2021/01/Executive_Summary_English_Web.pdf, 45.

[11] Aimée Craft, *Breathing Life into the Stone Fort Treaty: An Anishinaabe Understanding of Treaty One* (Saskatoon: Purich Publishing, 2013), 64.

and Indigenous oral histories, that the land surrender provision of the numbered treaties is invalid. Indigenous peoples never did agree to the land surrender clauses in the treaties.[12]

This conflict over the meaning of the treaties has roots even deeper than Columbus and his expedition of 1492. The Christianity that was the state religion throughout western Europe for centuries included a doctrine that non-Christians were subhuman unless they converted to the Europeans' one true faith. In 1455, Pope Nicholas V proclaimed the "Doctrine of Discovery," which purported to give land to European powers and authorized them to "invade, search out, capture, vanquish and subdue all enemies of Christ [and] reduce their persons to perpetual slavery."[13] Protestant nations such as England did not obey the Pope, but they happily adhered to similar principles.

In Canada, the British Crown negotiated many treaties affecting peoples in eastern Canada. After Confederation in 1867, the federal Canadian government negotiated 11 numbered treaties between 1871 and 1921 covering territory from Manitoba to British Columbia and the northern territories, more than half of Canada's total land mass today. Their primary purpose was to open land to settlement.

The Indian Act became law in 1876. Its primary purpose was to assimilate Indigenous peoples into settler culture, and it was the basis for the government-run residential school system that

---

[12] Sheldon Krasowski, *No Surrender: The Land Remains Indigenous* (Regina: University of Regina Press, 2019), 37.

[13] Steve Newcomb, "Five Hundred Years of Injustice: The Legacy of 15th Century Religious Prejudice," *Shaman's Drum*, fall 1992. Pope Francis finally rescinded the Doctrine of Discovery in 2023, after his trip to Canada in 2022 to apologize for the mistreatment of Indigenous peoples by Catholic priests and nuns.

began in 1883.[14] In a speech in the House of Commons, Prime Minister John A. Macdonald formally explained the role of residential schools. His comments and those made by others are summarized in what became a purpose statement for these so-called schools: "to kill the Indian in the child."[15] Numerous Christian churches collaborated with the government in running these institutions, which were actually prisons, since the inmates neither came nor stayed voluntarily. Priests and RCMP officers forcibly removed children from their families to cut them off from their language, culture, and religion in order to turn them into mainstream Canadians. These places were rife with disease and physical and sexual abuse. As of 2024, we know that over 7,600 children in these institutions died isolated from loved ones and were thrown into unmarked graves that are still being unearthed across Canada.[16]

The last residential school closed in 1996. Indigenous leaders fought the federal government to recognize that these schools had a devastating, multi-generational impact on Indigenous peoples. They finally reached a settlement with the government in 2008, which included an apology, financial compensation, and establishing the Truth and Reconciliation Commission. The TRC held 14 hearings across the country and issued its final report in 2015. That report documented the residential school experiences of 150,000 students. It called the system an act of "cultural genocide," because it resulted from a policy that deliberately tried to destroy the languages and cultures that are central to the lives and identities of Indigenous peoples.[17]

---

[14] Various churches operated and funded residential schools, often with government support, since 1831. https://www.thecanadianencyclopedia.ca/en/article/residential-schools

[15] https://ehprnh2mwo3.exactdn.com/wp-content/uploads/2021/01/Executive_Summary_English_Web.pdf, 2.

[16] For a concise list of the devastating and continuing impacts of The Indian Act, see Aaron Paquette's Foreword in this book.

[17] See https://nctr.ca/ the website of the National Centre for Truth and Reconciliation.

Canada's racist policies continue to hamper Indigenous peoples in the 21st century. The disproportionate numbers of Indigenous among Canada's poor, homeless, addicted, murdered, missing, and imprisoned is the direct result of those policies. The so-called "60s Scoop," during which government officials removed Indigenous children from their families and their cultures, was a new version of the residential school system. Child welfare staff put Indigenous children into white foster homes instead of residential schools.

The 60s Scoop sounds like it happened 60 years ago, but Indigenous children continue to be wards of child welfare in numbers proportionately far greater than settler children. And, to this day, governments' attempts to Indigenize child welfare have failed because those same governments grossly underfund the process. On October 23, 2023, the Federal Court awarded $23 billion to First Nations children and families "who experienced racial discrimination through Ottawa's chronic underfunding of the on-reserve foster care system and other family services."[18] Federal Conservative and Liberal governments have been fighting against Indigenous activist Cindy Blackstock's efforts to correct this injustice since 2007.[19] Obviously, these governments could not have sustained that fight if the voting public opposed it.

The beginning of this Introduction quotes the final report of the National Inquiry into Missing and Murdered Indigenous Women and Girls. Federal governments long resisted demands from various Indigenous groups and other Canadian and international organizations, like Amnesty International and the United Nations, to address the femicide consequence of widespread injustice toward Indigenous peoples. According to Statistics

---

[18] https://www.cbc.ca/news/politics/judge-approves-23-billion-first-nations-child-welfare-agreement-1.7006351
[19] https://fncaringsociety.com/

Canada, Indigenous women over 15 years old in 2004 were 3.5 times more likely to experience violence than non-Indigenous women, and the homicide rate between 1997 and 2000 was nearly seven times higher than for non-Indigenous women. Those rates have increased since then.[20] But this national inquiry only happened when the plight of Indigenous women and girls became a federal election issue in 2015.

Misogyny is endemic to many cultures. Its impact on Indigenous peoples since colonization has been profound. Many First Nations, Inuit, and Métis groups have had female leadership throughout their history, both as elders and as traditional officials. Euro-colonial, patriarchal governance models have undermined this traditional female leadership.

Violence against Indigenous women and girls has torn communities apart, disrupted families, and prevented healthy relationships. Nonetheless, Indigenous women are now reclaiming their power and taking up leadership roles again. Reconciliation efforts must recognize the injustices specific to Indigenous women and girls. Their very lives are at risk. However, as the MMIWG inquiry experience demonstrates, political pressure can achieve real change, and every Canadian has a responsibility to speak up and vote for justice.

How can land acknowledgements be a part of that effort? Land acknowledgments rarely suggest how settlers and their descendants should feel about occupying ancestral Indigenous lands or how to relate to Indigenous people today. Why not? This book provides some examples by both settler and Indigenous writers who do that and more. Of course, we must go far beyond land acknowledgements, no matter how sincere. But a land acknowledgement that requires the author first learn

---

[20] https://www.thecanadianencyclopedia.ca/en/article/missing-and-murdered-indigenous-women-and-girls-in-canada

the history and the current issues is a way to teach those things to others and an important step toward the better Canada we hope to create.

Here are some guidelines for everyone who has an opportunity to compose land acknowledgments.

First, do not try to summarize all the issues and all the facts in one acknowledgment. Pick one piece of the story. You can't do all of reconciliation at once. Use the resources in this book to become familiar with history and current events. Get more knowledge, and focus on one part of it that strikes a chord with you. Try to make one or two points well.

Second, examine your personal connections to the issues. Are you a recent settler in Canada, or did your grandparents or great-grandparents come here? Did they homestead land once occupied by herds of buffalo? Are you connected in some way to Indigenous history? Have you heard an Indigenous rock band that you like? Do you have a relationship to the land that is relevant? Do you "own" the land you live on? What does that mean today? If you are not connected with the Indigenous community, do you have a special relationship to the land where you live? How would you like to connect to the Indigenous community? How can you thank the Indigenous community for sharing their land?

Third, pick a genre that appeals to you. You can draft a poem, write a short essay, tell a story, sing a song, or write a letter. It can be short or long. This is your chance to do something different, something your group will remember and will later thank you for your imagination, your courage, your originality. With your help, land acknowledgments can become the foundation of a new, more equal, fairer, anti-racist Canada.

Fourth, suggest something real to your audience. You probably know who they are and whether they are interested in the issues. If they are not, suggest why Indigenous issues should matter to them. There might be an artist who creates silk-screen prints for gifts. Maybe there is an Indigenous craft store in your town. Is there an Indigenous-owned gas station nearby where interested drivers can support an Indigenous group by purchasing gas? Maybe an online company ships comfortable Indigenous-made moccasins to you. You can find these resources and help your listeners connect. Strike up a conversation with an Indigenous person. Attend an Indigenous celebration. Learn some Indigenous words and phrases.

Finally, make your land acknowledgment your own. Do not follow a formula. Do not cite fact after fact. Do not stress guilt and regret. Think of the future, of a better world for Indigenous people and settlers alike. Speak your land acknowledgment in your own voice. The land acknowledgments in this book are experiments. The writers explore the landscape, sometimes with great courage and sometimes more cautiously. You can go farther and speak your own version. You will then be part of that reconciliation we seek.

Of course, you will be writing for the people of the present. Many of these people are settlers who recognize the genocide of the past but fail to recognize any personal responsibility for the present circumstances of Indigenous people. Many don't even recognize that they live on land that is still Indigenous land. Many in your audience of settlers may suffer from a modern malady known as "white fragility."[21] This is the defensive and angry denial of the fact that they benefit from institutional racism. Most white people are good people who are offended by

---

[21] Robin DiAngelo, *White Fragility: Why It's So Hard for White People to Talk about Racism* (Toronto: Penguin-Random House Canada, 2018).

any suggestion that they might be racist. You can gently suggest that it may be time to reassess their beliefs.

"White fragility," for example, is why shaming, guilt-tripping, or blaming settlers for the present situation usually backfires. What may work, however, is focusing on how to improve today's circumstances for Indigenous people, finding ways to link Indigenous lives with the people in your audience, and looking at ways to create a better future: reconciliation.

Perhaps you can help your audience see ways they can help fix a flawed system in which Indigenous people on reserves cannot own the land they live on or even have a semblance of self-governance. Settlers as well as Indigenous people can work together to repeal the repressive Indian Act.

Your audience can learn from thoughtful leaders like you. They vote and can write letters to their representatives. They can support Indigenous businesses and political movements. They can enjoy Indigenous art, dance, and music. They can make a difference, and your land acknowledgment can help point the way.

Land Acknowledgments Project Committee
Leslie Y. Dawson, Janis Dow Durnin, Gary Garrison,
Naomi McIlwraith

Upon Whose Land Do You Stand?

Stefani Alzati

Names and power go hand in hand
as we honour the first people of this land.
Where now there are buildings and boxes
and parking garages
the land back then was untamed.
There were more names for rain (we will never hear)
because of what happened to the people
who have always been here,
nôhkum and nimosôm who planted and grew
so that we could have the lives that we do.

The First People toiled by hand,
stepping on forest floors with the lightest touch
stealthily navigating dense underbrush.
There were no machines to help,
only brotherhood and sisterhood and clan.
In those times the people of this land, nîsôhkamâtowak,
helped each other.
My clan, my grandparents were gifted stolen land
by the government (and not the Red Rock Indian Band).

Who lived on this land? Who lives on this land?
I say your name with gratitude, honour, and respect
for the gifts so openly shared.
nehiyawak Cree bring balance in four parts
through four directions, East, South, West, North.
Blackfoot share seven sacred teachings:
honesty, humility, truth, wisdom, love, respect, bravery.
Métis remind us to embrace life and celebrate
with music, language, and *joie de vivre*.
Nakota Sioux stone guardians are friends,
sharing secrets and ancient knowledge.

In Alberta today, over 46 Nations, nurturers, protectors,
and children who did not make it home.

Thank you for teaching us and protecting
these lands across Turtle Island
and here in amiskwaciy-wâskahikan (ᐊᒥᐢᑲᐧᒋᐩ ᐋᐧᐢᑲᐦᐃᑲᐣ),
in your spirit and animal form.
We’ve come a long way and we’ve got a long way to go
in this ongoing act of reconciliation.
nîsôhkamâtowak we help each other
nitohtamowin ᓂᑐᐦᑕᒧᐃᐧᐣ listening
wîcihitowin helping each other in a good way
so we can live together in harmony.[22]

[22] A version of this poem first appeared in the artist’s somatic poetry and visual art exhibit, *Poet Tree amener l’extérieur à l’intérieur at Centre d’arts visuels de l’Alberta* (CAVA), 2022.

Re-Imagining Our Connections

Hank Binnema

We live on Treaty 6 territory where Cree, Dene, Anishinabek, Métis, and Blackfoot have lived for millennia. They lived on the grasslands where they co-existed with buffalo and thrived as part of a living eco-system, the complexity of which I am only beginning to understand. Every year now, uncontrolled fires devastate the forests and grasslands of Treaty 6 territory and the surrounding lands of Turtle Island. I am all the more humbled to learn how Indigenous people knew how to use controlled fire to enhance the lives of themselves and all their relations. These beautiful grasslands and forests are now choked and surrounded by fences, walls, and restrictive border policies. Fences now corral so many who used to roam freely and knew how to survive and thrive in the long winters and summers of the vast, open prairie winds.

I came to this territory as a six-year-old child from the Netherlands. Certainly, many of us there loved the land as Indigenous people here do, albeit using different methods. Unfortunately, we are also responsible for genocides of Indigenous nations in other parts of the world. For example, in 1621, Dutch soldiers almost completely obliterated the people of Banda Islands, a group of islands in the South Moluccas in what is now Indonesia. (Today, descendants of the Banda people ethnically cleansed by the Dutch don't live on Banda Islands; they live on nearby islands in Indonesia or they live in the Netherlands.)

At the same time, half-way across the world, Dutch soldiers built a wall to keep away the Lenape people in what is now called New York. Today, that street is called Wall Street, which is home to money changers whose spiraling bargains threaten to spin our whole world out of control.

In the aftermath of a brutal war, many of us came to a new land unaware of who the people were that we were displacing. Today, we need their wisdom more than ever, as Indigenous people around the world are still being displaced. We not only have abandoned bones surrounding former residential schools, we are piling on abandoned bones by means of our borders, barbed wire fences, walls, and demagogic border policies.

Let's together make a promise: a renewed and expanded Treaty 6 that truly includes the knowledge and wisdom of the Cree, Dene, Anishinabek, Métis, and Blackfoot who have lived in these lands for millennia.

A Homesteader's Land Acknowledgement

Audrey Brooks

My mother often talked about what it was like to be a homesteader in Saskatchewan when she was a young girl. Her parents were Hungarian immigrants who were told by the Canadian government that if they could clear land and build a house on it, they would receive title to that land. Her father talked about how their family would never have survived their first winter in Canada if it hadn't been for the Indians. Immigrants knew nothing about how to prepare for winter. Their shacks were made of green logs that let in the cold, and the mud they used to fill in the cracks froze. He said that at first, the Indians and the Hungarians could not communicate with each other, but the Indians knew there was big trouble on that homestead and would turn up with frozen moose meat and plants that made hot tea. Over time, some kind of relationship happened.

Mother said that when she was a kid, the Indian family travelled along their road every year when they moved to their summer campground. One year the grandfather of the chief died, and the chief asked her dad if he could be buried outside our fence, and not to plow it there. Her dad told him, "As long as our family holds this land, we won't plow it under." The cattle fence was built behind the grave so the cows wouldn't trample it. Her mother used to send her to tend the grave. She was given a pail of loam to dig into the ground around the grave in the spring, then planted wildflowers there.

My mother said, "The Indians visited the grave every year, stopping to eat food and rest. Their visits coincided with the migration of game. When Indian berries showed dark red on the bushes, when the wild mushrooms and herbs were ready for picking, those Indians appeared. When I was sent to tend the grave, it meant no more to me than digging up asparagus or weeding the strawberry field. It was part of my chores. Every year, my dad would grow extra vegetables, and the Indians would exchange wild game for them."

"The farmers wanted the police to get rid of the Indians from the land," she said, "because they were afraid of them. So, the RCMP officer by the name of Noll told my dad the Indians had to be off our land by spring. Our town was a weird place in those days. People made up stories about Indians that they believed themselves. But, like my dad said, we got more help from our Indian friends than wc did from the people in town. The Indians were like us. They loved their kids. They knew how to share. We didn't know when we first came out here that the government didn't own the land we were on."

My mother often said that the Indians and her family were "in this together." Both families lived off the land, in very challenging times.

The Secret Pre-History of Cobalt, Ontario

David Brydges

I live in the Temiskaming District Treaty 9 territory. The lands are the traditional territory of Ojibwe/Chippewa, Mushkegowuk (Cree), Algonquin, and Métis peoples.

For thousands of years before treaties artificially carved scars in the land and its Indigenous peoples, a foreign god's bible told newcomers to "go forth and multiply." Gitchi Manitou, the great spirit of the Ojibwa, proclaims a larger truth that says to let nature go forth, and it will multiply all you need when you respect its spirit. This is wisdom we need today.

Long before the prospectors descended on Cobalt, Indigenous peoples found silver trinkets under the local lake's surface and traded them as far away as Ohio. They would not say where that lake lay. There was a superstition that misfortune would follow should they reveal its hiding place.

Surveyors in 1900 came across a lake called Mesinochwanigwahghaning, meaning, "the lake with the soft rock which can be written upon." They decided this Algonquin name was too long and called the body of water Peter Long Lake.

In my hometown of Cobalt, silver was discovered in 1903. The provincial geologist W.G. Miller changed its name to Cobalt Lake. I am working on a reconciliation project to install a plaque near the lake with its original Indigenous name and story.

Names

Kayleigh Cline

In 2011-12, I was honoured to take two semesters of "Introductory Cree" with Dorothy Thunder at the University of Alberta. I entered the classroom expecting to work hard—I have no gift for languages—but I was determined to dive into the anxiety. Dorothy's warmth, kindness, and neverending patience made it easy, which I know many of those in the Edmonton area who have taken her classes can attest to.

In those early classroom days, I realized that learning Cree was the first time I was learning a language that had come from this place many of us now call Edmonton. These were words that were born here, that fit this place in a way that simply made sense in a way that my English words did not. My globalized English takes its words from so many places, endlessly re-purposing words and sounds for new meanings and contexts.

Cree keeps its etymologies close. My favourite example was the poster of colour words that hung on the classroom door, which showed that to call something "green" in Cree, you say it is "land-coloured" (askihtakosiw/askihtakwâw). Technically, English does this too. I can Google that the origin of the word "green" is "groene," which is Northumbrian for "the color of growing plants." But how many English speakers know this? Or think about this in their everyday use? In Cree class, knowing the word for "land" was fundamentally a part of learning what it meant to be "green."

Poetry does this too: metaphorizing, personifying, defamiliarizing, and all those other neat tricks to bring us back to remembering what language can do because of what it becomes when it leaps off our tongues and our pages to be in the real world.

And what is an “Edmonton” anyhow? The Cree name for this land is amiskwaciy-wâskahikan, which is made up of the words that translate into English as “Beaver Hills House.” A name to describe the river embankment I could walk past after class and the poplars hourglassed by beaver teeth along those same trails. A name that remembers the fort. A name that makes sense for this place. A name that tells the poetry of this place.

There are other names for this place too: omahkoyis (Niitsitapi), nasagachoo (Tsuut’ina), ti oda (Nakota Sioux), Forts des Prairies (French-Métis). These names use the fort as a place where people gather. Like we are today. So, today, I ask you to honour those who know this place, who have gifted this place with these names, as well as others who have gathered in this place: the nêhiyaw, Denesuliné, Anishinaabe, Nakota Sioux, Niitsitapi, Métis, and Inuit peoples.

Land acknowledgements are made of words which, by themselves, are not enough. Words and actions need to walk together, side by side, so that when we stumble, words can help us back onto the path. Remember these names and the people who speak them as you walk through this place.

Marking the Boundaries

Leslie Dawson

It took 80 years after the signing of Treaty 6 for the Canadian government to get around to officially surveying the boundaries of the Hobbema Indian Reserves. When they did, they sent a young man from Ontario, Donald K. F. Dawson, to survey the land. He was about 30 years old, a veteran of World War II, with a young wife, Nancy, and two small children, me and my brother Eric.

Dad took the train out to Hobbema—now maskwacîs—and took up residence in the Indian agent's white, clapboard house. As an official agent of the federal government, my dad's job was to physically mark, with iron stakes, the boundaries of the reserves, to indicate the exact limits of the land reserved for the First Nations people. His marks showed where they could settle, hunt, celebrate their ceremonies, and till the soil: where they could live. And he showed the exact limits of white settlers' lands, which surrounded the First Nations people on every side. After a few months, mom and I and Eric took the train from Ontario to join my father in Hobbema. Dad met us at the station in the middle of the night and took us to our new home.

As a colonial officer, my dad was sensitive and liberal-minded for the times. He said he never set foot on sacred places, including the burial grounds. He hired young men of the nation for his crew, giving some of them their first official jobs in the white man's world. Dad kept those men on his crew for years afterwards. He made sure they were properly paid.

George Wildcat was one of the men. George made me a bow and arrows. He took me to a prairie field and showed me how to draw back the bow and shoot. I remember his gift and his lesson so clearly. His widow came to my father's funeral many years later.

As a child, my life in maskwacîs was an idyll. I have a happy memory of sitting on the ground, playing in the dirt in front of the Hobbema general store. Four or five elders sat on a bench under the awning, quietly conversing in Cree while the sun shone vividly across the road on fields of wheat behind the grain elevator and the railway tracks. I remember feeling the kindness of the old men, their calm acceptance of this three-year-old child at their feet, whose father was drawing the straight lines, the boundaries around them, these men who had once roamed free for a thousand miles following the buffalo, the entire prairies their domain.

My father banged in the final nails of Treaty 6 for them. It was no big deal at the time, just a bureaucratic afterthought for a people long since conquered, or so everyone thought.

But I remember. I remember those old men, once kings of the land, sitting with their memories, on this land. Their children now know that this is still their land, and we, like my father and his family, are guests here. I remember that the wind blows across this land, the sun and the moon shine upon it, and George Wildcat's grandchildren still live here.

And now, I am a grateful guest here, grateful that the people of maskwacîs share their land with me, grateful for a life lived under the great, azure sky, on their magnificent prairies.

That is how I remember Treaty 6.

On Being So Ignorant

Leslie Dawson

Years ago—so many years ago—I was charged with researching the history of Elk Island National Park. Nothing had been written. We knew only the names of a few homesteaders who had settled on the land. A few of these old timers still survived. Eventually though, I ended up on a nearby Indigenous reserve, talking to some descendants of the park's original people.

It was spring. The people, an old woman and an old man, greeted me with quiet hospitality. They prepared bannock for me and made afternoon tea. I saw bearskin blankets hanging out in the warm air to freshen up. The old people told me the meaning of place names in the park. They knew the land. Elk Island, like all the lands around me, was an Indigenous hunting ground before the settlers came. It was a Cree place, the Beaver Hills, a good place to hunt big game and bison and to trap for furs. There was fresh water in the many lakes and streams. But above all, it was Indigenous land.

Now, I think back to my innocent, ignorant inquiries. I was just 20 years old and knew nothing. Nothing about Indigenous history, nothing about residential schools, and nothing about the treaties. I had rolled in on my red motorcycle and simply assumed the people had led uneventful lives like mine. I was like most of the settlers on treaty lands, even today. How could I have been so innocent of centuries of conquering, decades of genocide, generations of racism? We had learned nothing in school and nothing through the media.

So, yes, I was innocent and definitely ignorant. But there's no excuse for it now. We've had national inquiries and huge reports. Indigenous people themselves are fighting loudly for their identity and rights. I see Indigenous history on Facebook and hear their stories on TV and radio. Many Indigenous writers are being published. And sadly, the gravesites of thousands of children have sprung up all around us. So much grief, so many brief lives.

I would go, today, into that Indigenous village a different woman: quietly, humbled, and carrying the burden of colonial history. And today, I know that this land where I live and work is not mine. I walk and drive on ancient paths marked by ancient peoples.

Tonight, I acknowledge these lands, and their peoples. It is the very least I can do. And I look for concrete ways to reconcile the past with today's realities.

The First Poets Here Were Indigenous

Leslie Dawson

We are meeting tonight on the land whose traditional community was the Indigenous peoples named in Treaty 6, a sacred agreement between the British Crown and a huge group of Indigenous communities.

I can imagine these peoples meeting here, down by the river, for hundreds of years, singing their own poetry into the valleys and plains, drumming their songs into the prairie skies. Can you hear their cries? Can you imagine their voices?

We latter-day poets sing more quietly, our feet on their land, our voices only remembering their dances. But they were the first poets here, crying out to the sun and the stars, as we do sometimes, remembering without realizing, our connections to the land and the sky and the rivers.

We thank the peoples of Treaty 6 for their first poems and songs. And tonight, we share their land with respect and humility.

Mvskoke Motherland

Dr. Deidra Suwanee Dees

crystal clear
water swirls
around my feet,

regenerative soil
gives

life-nourishing
abundance,

moss laden live oaks

provide Garden-
of-Eden
coolness,

richness of
Mother Earth

sustains generations
of millions

where my ancestors
lived

out their
permanency

protecting Mvskoke motherland
with all of their

lifeforce;

motherland where
my feet

stand
firmly planted today

The Land You Live On

Dr. Deidra Suwanee Dees

you killed my grandmother
to stop future brownskin babies from
being born
on my motherland

who would remind you
the land you live on
is stolen,
the faces you paint on your
currency
are liars,

the people you descend from
are murderers;

you drink in a cup of jesus on sunday
in the heart of my motherland—
it is my blood you drink!
to fill your belly
with nourishment
of manifest destiny;

you cough up articulate
land
acknowledgement statements

but you do not acknowledge

how fat you have grown
          on juices of jesus,
manifest destiny,
          and brownskin babies

Prairie Connections

Janis Dow Durnin

For our Treaty 6 land acknowledgment today[23] I want to share a personal memory with you. I come from the southwestern Manitoba prairies where, with my grandmother, mother, and siblings, I searched for crocuses and tipi rings on the wide-open prairie in the spring. Tipi rings are rocks that held down the tipis and form a circle where the base was.

For us kids, looking for tipi rings was like finding clues on a treasure hunt beyond time. It was exciting, and when we found one we would shout, and my grandmother and my mom would come and look at it and say, "Yes, that looks like one," or "No, it's not." This is a fond memory for me, being on the wide-open prairie where Indigenous peoples once lived and buffalo roamed free, and it left me with a feeling of connection to the land. By association, I also felt connected to the First Peoples who walked, lived, and cared for the land long ago.

I am grateful for the Indigenous peoples who continue to inhabit Canada today and their teachings which encourage stewardship of the land and respect for all beings within the greater circle of life we're all a part of.

---

[23] First presented as mic host at the beginning of the Poets Haven poetry reading series held by the Stroll of Poets, September 2022.

First Nation Footsteps

Janis Dow Durnin

We come to you today from Treaty 6 territory where the first people to walk this land were the First Nations peoples. Their footsteps and way of life blessed this land that we now call home.

I listen in my heart for their song, I acknowledge the dark drumbeats of the past, and I build bridges of compassion by listening to their stories with an open heart. I honor their teachings, the spirit of the land, and all our relations, of which we're all a part.

Gratitude First

Janis Dow Durnin

We would like to acknowledge that we are on Treaty 6 territory. This means different things to different people. In recognition of the fact that we live on Treaty 6 territory, today I'll read a portion of the Onondaga Nation's "Thanksgiving address." The Onondaga people live in what is now called the state of New York. Their "Thanksgiving address" is known more accurately as "The Words That Come Before All Else" in the Onondaga language and sets gratitude as the highest priority.

This excerpt appears in Robin Wall Kimmerer's book *Braiding Sweetgrass*. The scene is a school on Onondaga Nation land. In front of the school flies the purple and white flag of the Haudenosaunee Confederacy. The school week begins and ends with the entire student body assembled in the school atrium. It is the third grade's turn to recite the address in the Onondaga language, their mother tongue, which the other students repeat back to them.

> Today we have gathered and when we look upon the faces around us we see that the cycles of life continue. We have been given the duty to live in balance and harmony with each other and all living things. So now let us bring our minds together as one as we give greetings and thanks to each other as People. Now our minds are one.[24]

---

[24] Robin Wall Kimmerer, *Braiding Sweetgrass: Indigenous Wisdom, Scientific Knowledge, and the Teachings of Plants* (Minneapolis: Milkweed Editions, 2013), 107. A footnote in the book says, "The actual wording of the Thanksgiving Address varies with the speaker. This text is the widely publicised version of John Stokes and Kanawahientun, 1993."

Terrible Truths

Janis Dow Durnin

Not long after the remains of 215 children were found on the grounds of a residential school in Kamloops, B.C., in 2021, I had a conversation with an Indigenous acquaintance from the Hobbema reserve. As the shock, horror, and shame of my European ancestors' actions began to settle into me, I defensively said to an Indigenous acquaintance, "What do you want from us?" Part of that difficult interaction was her reply, "We won't see this healed in our lifetime."

Little did I know that her words would start a crack in the whitewashed window pane of fragility I'd seen things through for many years. Her candor set me on a path to break open Canada's true history and the impact of colonialism on Indigenous Peoples on Turtle Island, not the half-truths I'd learned about Canada in history class.

In the three years since then, I've had many conversations with the wise and knowledgeable members of the Stroll of Poets committee who I have collaborated with to create this book. I've had conversations as well with a Cree Elder, her daughter, and others. These have helped me understand the very real, destructive impact colonialism has had and continues to have on the Indigenous peoples of this land. It has robbed Indigenous peoples of their original ways of life, their language, their children, their culture, and their rights to exist, fully, as the Creator made them, on the land where they were born and to which the rest of us came, uninvited.

Colonialism is the foundation of our society, a society of inequity and injustice on so many levels: mental, physical, emotional, social, financial, and ecological.

I was surprised and humbled to learn many facts I only had an inkling of before. I had to listen bravely and let go of what I thought I knew. I yearned yet feared to empathize with the Indigenous peoples' grief after so many decades of genocide and mistreatment on the land we settlers call Canada.

The grief, shock, shame, and despondency I felt became a gift. I learned to be more authentic about my feelings and to listen in my heart for what Indigenous people are saying and to own personally the heinous actions of my ancestors. That gift prompts me to contribute what I can to help heal Indigenous peoples' pain and look for ways to create an anti-racist country.

I now understand that it's important to acknowledge the past, to write about it, and to take action where I can. For instance, I no longer stand up for "O Canada" when it's played, nor do I sing along with the lyrics, as there is no mention of Indigenous peoples in it anywhere, nor any acknowledgement of Canada's history of racism, which continues to this day.

Facing the truth about Canada's colonialism and racism is painful for me, but I am committed to speaking that truth to others, no matter how uncomfortable that is. If each of us settlers would take small steps to learn our history and collaborate with Indigenous peoples to celebrate their cultures and their diversity, we would start to create a new society, a future where we can all live as equals, where racism and injustice have no place to hide.

Stride for Stride

Douglas Elves

We stand where First Nations walked,
but find we cannot remember the way
unless we walk beside them.

This Land

Lynn Gale

When I was a little girl, I remember listening to the song "This Land is My Land" and hearing in the lyrics, "this land was made for you and me." But that isn't the whole truth, is it?

I was not born here, on this land. I was born in France, to parents in the Canadian Armed Forces. My parents were born in Canada, but their parents were not. Yet we have always taken it as our unspoken right that this land is our land.

It is not our land. It is not my land. It was made for and by those who came before us, who travel now in shadows, in memories, and in dreams. It is their land.

We are grateful to recognize that we are following in the footsteps of the many First Nations, Métis, and Inuit whose footsteps have marked these lands for generations. Their echoes reverberate through this land, sharing their story with those who will listen.

We are grateful for the traditional knowledge keepers and elders who are still with us today and those who have gone before us.

We acknowledge that we are on Treaty 6 territory, a traditional meeting ground, gathering place, and traveling route for the Cree, Saulteaux, Blackfoot, Métis, Dene, and Nakota Sioux.

We are learning to listen, to remember, to be grateful, and to allow the voices previously silenced to be heard.

We are learning to be respectful, kind, and compassionate.

We are learning.

Genocide: Never Again

Gary Garrison

Canada began as crooked lines on a map, as script on company charters, as words in British and French laws, as ink on handwritten treaties. Surveyors' stakes, creosoted ties, steel rails, trestles, and bridges crossed vast distances to make those words and lines fact on the land. They brought settlers with their police, their machinery, their languages, and their religions. People came from Britain and France and then from the United States, Africa, China, and all over the world to build cities, towns, homesteads, highways, economies that we all participate in to this day.

We call this land Canada, but the land was here long before there was a Canada. The land was home to hundreds of languages, cultures, spiritual practices, communities, and civilizations as advanced as any in Europe. We call this land's people Aboriginal because, as they themselves say, they have been here from time immemorial, from the beginning.[25] Everything about their daily lives— their languages, religions, medicines, stories, food, and their very bodies—grew out of the land itself, just as trees do. Their descendants still embody that connection, despite five centuries of settlers' efforts to sever it, efforts not only to take their land but, in fact, to tear apart their families and to exterminate them as nations—the very definition of genocide—and to force the survivors to live our way of life or die.

Some believe the way to reverse this injustice is to tear down statues of Canada's founders, like Sir John A. Macdonald, who

---

[25] Scientists say they migrated from Asia, across the Bering Strait, but questions remain about whether that happened 20 or 130 millennia or more ago and whether some came to South America across the Pacific. See https://www.cbc.ca/radio/ideas/indigenous-archaeologist-argues-humans-may-have-arrived-here-130-000-years-ago-1.6313892

built the railroad and the residential school system. I say we need those statues, that steel rail, and those brick buildings to remind us settlers and settler descendants that Canada is not an idyllic, pure, red-and-white maple leaf flag rippling in the wind but a country with blood on its hands even as it professes to have justice in its heart.

The Canada I want to leave for my grandchildren and their grandchildren is a country that knows its history, respects the land, and honours the people who have always been part of it, to honour First Nations peoples not as quaint artifacts but as teachers whose ancient wisdom we need to mentor us in caring for this land, its soil, air, plants, animals, and water for as long as its rivers flow.

The first step is to recognize the dishonourable side of our country's history, to imagine, for example, what we would do if police and clergymen stole children from our families, punished them when they spoke our language or practiced our religion, kept them apart from their parents, and buried them in unmarked graves.

What would we do if that same government kept taking our children away for seven generations because most of us were raised outside our culture, away from our families, and never had a chance to learn positive parenting skills? Where would that leave us? How could we not end up with intergenerational trauma? Kidnapping our children would be enough by itself to cause profound dysfunction among us, even if our ancestral lands were not stolen, even if nobody punished us for speaking our language and practicing our religion, and even if we weren't the butt of racist jokes and racist government policies.

Resurrection

Gary Garrison

When Canada is just a baby, he believes
he can have it all, sea to sea to sea.
The land is empty but for beasts and forests.
Those biped imposters can't be human
for they are brown and unbaptized,
speak in gibberish, wear feathers,
worship smoke, birds, and trees.
So, he draws lines on parchment,
fingerpaints his front and back yards
full of farmhouses and barns, villages and cities.
He gets a train set, builds bridges and trestles,
blows up mountains, digs tunnels, lays tracks.
He gazes at locomotives, passenger cars
full of settlers to drop off on the prairies.
He dreams airports, oil wells, diamond mines,
sawmills, pulp mills, office towers, and seaports,
ships full of crude, wheat, beef, and lumber
crossing oceans. Cyber banks full of cyber gold.

As an adult, he sees himself equal to Rome, Britain,
China, Russia, the U.S., but with better healthcare,
more political parties, and gun-violence free.
He builds statues, monuments to honour himself,
hosts lavish fireworks parties on his birthday.
When those impostors' children's bones
rise again and again from the dirt,
in B.C., Alberta, Saskatchewan, Ontario,
he wonders how they came back, and why.
His priests taught him they had no souls,
and he believed them, for he wanted the land,
And Christ died for *him*. He knew he was right
to take them from parents, to kill their gibberish

and the smoke, birds, and trees they worshipped.

He meant well. He didn't shoot them. Everybody dies.
These ghosts demand their land, but it's his.
His parents' royal seals and laws prove it.
More and more of them rise from the soil.
Their nieces and nephews also rise up.
They say they have papers with royal seals too,
and they are many nations. But Canada,
he dithers. Provincial autonomy, climate change,
minority government, foreign wars, inflation . . .
So he decrees that everywhere, everyone
on this land will acknowledge that the ghosts
owned the place first. But those old bones
keep rising up. Those voices keep shouting.

Buried Truths

Gary Garrison

People flocked to this land from abroad
with their guns, their trains, and their gods.
They took forests, rivers, mountains, prairies.
The locals' children, they stole and buried,
unmarked, near Christian boarding school facades.

Settler children learn the land is theirs,
the rocks, the trees, the water, the air,
that Indigenous people, unbaptized,
have chosen the Prince of Lies
and homeless lives of drunken despair.

The Canada they founded pretends
it's a nation where Jesus defends
the poor, the foreigner, children, the lame,
yet they make laws in his holy name
to imprison those they call "Indians."

"But those exhumed children's bones!"
they say. "Our children died too, at home,
of TB, of cholera, and the flu.
We'll all die sometime. *That's* news?"
These died kidnapped, abused, and alone.

"Get over it," they say. "That's history."
But who wrote the books? Not Blackfoot or Cree.
Who wrote treaties to expropriate land
in language the locals couldn't understand?
Who indoctrinates kids and says they're free?

It's 2120. Gods old and new
weave a tapestry red, yellow, black, blue,

a polyglot nation where water and stone
are honoured as people, no one’s alone,
and nobody buries whatever is true.

Speaking the names

Trudy Grienauer

As we begin, we wish to acknowledge that the land on which most of us live, and on which this building is located, is Treaty 6 territory, a traditional meeting ground and home for many Indigenous peoples, including Cree, Saulteaux, Blackfoot, Métis, and Nakota Sioux.

We acknowledge that traditional land recognition is an important first step towards reconciliation and justice. We encourage everyone to examine what we can do individually and in community to create an equitable relationship with our First Nations neighbours.

One small step, but I think an important one, is to learn the pronunciation of Indigenous place names. Edmonton's name in the Cree language is amiskwaciy-wâskahikan [AH-MI-S-KWA-CEE-WÂ-S-KA-HI-KA-N], meaning Beaver Hills House. In 2020, our city wards received new Indigenous names. Ward 10, where this building is located, is now called Ipiihkoohkanipiaohtsi [E-PEE-KO-KA-NEE PIU-TSI-YA], meaning the traditional lands where the Blackfoot Nation performed buffalo rounds. My own ward is called pâhpâstêw [PÂ-PÂ-S-TE-W] after a highly respected leader of papaschase band 136. It also means "large woodpecker." You can find all ward names on the City of Edmonton website, www.edmonton.ca.

Learn What Happened. Reflect. Do Something.

Trudy Grienauer

We acknowledge that we are treaty people of Treaty 6 and are meeting on the traditional territory of the Blackfoot and Cree people, as well as other First Nations and Métis. I am particularly interested in local history, wondering who was before us right here.

This area is now part of the Edmonton ward pâhpâstêw, named for Chief Papaschase who settled in this area in the second half of the 1800s. He and his brother were signatories of Treaty 6 in 1877, but they were not assigned a reserve until three years later.

Papaschase wanted to settle between Mill Creek and Mount Pleasant, but instead was assigned land that is now Mill Woods. Only a few years later, the band was forced to give up the land when settlers petitioned the government to move the reserve away from Edmonton. The band dispersed; speculators bought the land and re-sold it to settlers.

Poets write many beautiful words about reconciliation, but sometimes we have to talk about plain old money. How much profit was made at the expense of starving and desperate First Nations and Métis?

A direct act of reconciliation is to support First Nations businesses with your purchases. The Papaschase band has re-formed itself and now owns a gas station on Gateway Boulevard. Now that I know more about their ancestors' history and their fight for compensation, I'm going to fill up there whenever I drive that way.

May they thrive.

This Sacred Land

Lois Mary Hammond

Tonight, I honour two wise and courageous elders from the Fireweed Clan in a Gitxsan community near Hazelton, B.C. Almost 40 years ago, Vi Smith and Marie Wilson became self-educated linguists and historians who took on the federal government to establish Gitxsan rights to ancestral lands, based on archival and oral history. Ottawa was surprised when these intelligent, fiercely determined grandmothers showed up, sometimes laughing at the officials, sometimes laughing at themselves.

Vi Smith and Marie Wilson taught me that, for Indigenous people, land is not about private ownership; it's about community and stewardship. "We hold a covenant with this land," said Vi. "It is ours to care for, whatever is left. Other people can leave, but we can't."

They taught me that land is about the sacred interconnection of all living things. We inhabit the Earth and Mother Earth inhabits us. Having a place to sit in the circle on the land is to be alive.

Tonight, I remember other Indigenous people I've known in person or on the written page, such as local authors Norma Dunning and Richard Van Camp and our own strolling poets. They teach us how to see and how to listen. They show us the life-giving power of spirit, community, story-telling, and laughter.

Now, here we are in this room, most of us descendants of colonial settlers who, for complicated reasons, are often estranged from Mother Earth and from the descendants of the First Peoples who lived and died here on Treaty 6 territory for millennia. This was the land of the Cree, Blackfoot, Nakota

Sioux, Dene, Saulteaux, Anishinaabe, and other First Nations. It's also the ancestral home of Inuit and Métis.

Sadly, so many of us have forgotten how to know the land and each other. We're unsure how to move forward from historical injustices and how to right present-day injustices. But, in a moment of silence, together we can strengthen our intent to do so.

(Silence)

It is a beginning.

Thank you.

A lifetime's journey

Trevor Hughes

I grew up in Liverpool, England, as many of you will know, and it's been a lifetime's journey for me leading to my arrival here in ward pâhpâstêw, Edmonton. I still feel very attached to the city of my birth, the warmth and sharp wit of its people, and the famous Liver Birds on the waterfront greeting those who approach by sea.

One thing I was dimly aware of in childhood was that Liverpool had a significant part to play in the slave trade in former times, though in a sanitized way. It was part of British colonial history, after all. I was, in effect, unwittingly part of a culture that exploited others without really comprehending the impact on those people.

During the late 1960s I first heard the music of Canadian-American singer Buffy Sainte-Marie. I was moved by her powerful denunciation of the way Indigenous people had been disinherited and their culture disregarded, especially in the powerful protest song, "Now That the Buffalo's Gone." It was quite an awakening for me and showed history from a different perspective, that of the dispossessed. It felt very special to hear her perform this song in Edmonton a few years ago on one of our annual visits.

I didn't imagine I would eventually end up living here, by way of several years spent in France, but it seems wholly appropriate that I should acknowledge my debt to all those Indigenous peoples who have lived on and nurtured this Treaty 6 territory which we are privileged to share today.

P.S. I am aware that Buffy Sainte-Marie's claims of First Nation ancestry have been recently called into question, but that does not alter the impact her song had on me at the time with regard to my awareness of the exploitation of Indigenous people.

Truth and Reconciliation

Melle Huizinga

Truth Telling
Freeing from bondage of fear
Release from chains of hurt
Relief from dammed up tears
Reprieve from penned up anger
The telling of truth breaks the prison of silence
In telling the truth, healing nurtures hope

Truth Listening
An opening of the heart
A sharing of the pain
An acceptance of anger
Setting aside judgement
Truth listening will unsettle the settler
with his burden of aboriginal guilt

Reconciliation and Restoration
In the cauldron of Canada we will
Forge and maintain respectful relations
The settler accepts that suffering can birth nobility[26]
But deceit births only deceit and remorse rights no wrongs
Apologies become burst balloons, jetsam of a political hangover

A Forward Path
Hearing with a new heart the truth of the story
Welcoming the painful gift of tears
Honouring the sacred ceremonies
Walking together in humility to share Creator's goodness
To regain honour as we share the land

---

[26] Editor's note: The belief that "suffering can birth nobility" is Judaeo-Christian, not Indigenous.

Growing a profusion of respect in Creator's garden
For the healing of all

Land Acknowledgement

Dan Knauss

In the past, I have written many things that acknowledge land and landscapes for their deep memories and the mark they make on the people who pass through them, but I haven't made a land acknowledgment as such until now.

It is important to name the people of this land called Beaver Hills House before its colonization and theirs— the nêhiyawak, Tsuut'ina, Anihšināpē, Niitsitapi, Michif PiYii, and Hohe Nakota. It's important because they are the last of its stewards who know how to sustain their families for many generations without exhausting the land or each other, even when they fight. It is one thing to steal land and another to destroy its capacity to give and support life at all. This is happening.

Have you noticed we are driving stolen cars? Screens and Zooms are the negation of embodied, common life on the land. The materials and energy they require are straining the carrying capacity of the earth that supports our lives.

Have you noticed that most land acknowledgments do not say much about the land? Land you can see, hear, smell, feel, and taste! Did you get your hands in the soil today? Did you smell the recent rainfall on dry soil?

Have you noticed that many land acknowledgments refer to amiskwaciy-wâskahikan as "a traditional meeting ground and home for many Indigenous peoples"? It is still a meeting ground and home for everyone who is here, but this word "traditional" suggests the meeting and home-making is all in the past or was then in its prime.

When a living culture has been pushed near extinction or is truly dead, its crafts, music, knowledge, and languages become "traditional," something attenuated and fragile that can be extracted in bits, turned into museum pieces to collect or items to sell. The traditional can be a part-time living for some, but it is a hard thing to put back into everyday use. Land can never be "traditional" like that. When it dies, so will we. Until then, it is living and giving life, as the grandmothers and grandfathers of the world intended. I would acknowledge this living, wounded, dying land.

This is what the Oglala Lakota holy man Heȟáka Sápa said even though he saw the great sickness of the world, that every little thing is sent for something, and in that thing, there should be happiness and the power to make happy. Like the grasses showing tender faces to each other, we should do the same, for this was the wish of the grandparents of the world.

Have the grasses shown you their faces today? Have you heard the wind in them? Let's acknowledge these things that are alive and happy still. What does it mean to listen to a land and its people? What can we receive if we are open to each other?

As I set roots down into this earth

Josephine LoRe

I am first generation on this land, this place now known as Calgary. My parents left Sicily to seek better opportunities for themselves and their children. I respectfully and humbly acknowledge that these lands where I live and create, Mohkinsstsis, this confluence of rivers, were originally inhabited and traversed for centuries by the Piikani, Siksika, Kainai, Tsuut'ina, Nakota, and Dene peoples, their antecedents and their descendants.

The place where I was born and raised, Toronto, "trees standing in water," is the land of many peoples including the Haudenosaunee, the Anishinaabe, the Mississauga, the Chippewa, and the Wendat.

I am grateful to these peoples for having brought language and poetry to this land, and I engage to embody their values, stewardship and sense of oneness with the Earth.

Shared Treasures

Dorothy Lowrie

In the treasures of my childhood
An intricately beaded necklace
With a heart and an eagle
Symbols of life, peace, and strength.
In the treasures of my childhood
A cradle made of bark
With a tiny oskawâsis
Swaddled, warm and safe.

In the treasures of my childhood
Feathers, white and blue
Stones polished by streams that sparkle
Gifts from Mother Earth.
These things I chose to treasure
Without knowing Indigenous ways
My soul was drawn to them
Now I read and listen and shed tears
Learning how your treasures
Were torn from you.
I reach out my hands
That we might share these treasures
Love of heart, the symbol of life
Love of an eagle, the symbol of peace and strength
Love of a child, growing up warm and safe
Love of feathers and stones, from our sacred earth.

With reconciliation and gratitude, we recognize the wonderful treasures of the culture and lands of Alberta's Indigenous people, subject to treaties 6, 7, and 8. This includes tribes of the Blackfoot Confederacy, the Cree, the Dene, Saulteaux, Nakota Sioux, Stoney Nakota, the Tsuut'ina Nation, and the Métis people of Alberta. We acknowledge the many First Nations,

Métis, and Inuit who have lived in and cared for this land for generations. May we all open our hands and hearts and learn from each other how to protect our treasures for the future.

The continuing conversation

Alice Major

Poetry is a conversation between past and present.

I came to what we now call Treaty 6 territory four decades ago, not really expecting to be here for long. However, this place spoke to me and I stayed. But at the beginning, I knew little of the peoples who had lived here for thousands of years or of the complicated history of European settlement and the wrongs that were done in that process. It has been a one-sided conversation for too long.

Slowly we are becoming aware of the unattended-to sides of the story. Personally, I am so grateful to have found this place that offered space for me to write poetry, a place where stories, songs, and prayers have been composed and spoken for millennia. I hope we can continue a conversation with Indigenous people so that, together, we make space for all our voices, in the present and into the future.

What Land Acknowledgements Mean to Me

Lavona McIlwraith

Reflecting on the meaning of land acknowledgements immediately takes me back to age six when I first began experiencing life as an Indigenous person but didn't know it. I did not know that I was different from other children, because my parents didn't discuss my heritage before I started school, during my growing years, or after. Through the years, I was unprepared for the numerous incidents of racism I've endured in my life, but who really is prepared for such meanness? I will mention two or three of these demoralizing episodes.

On the way home from school at the age of six, I received a beating from two older boys who also called me a "dirty little Indian." I ran home crying to ask my mother, "What is an Indian?" I don't remember her answer. They beat me a second time, and my mother went to the mother of one of the boys to solve the problem. We lived on Halifax Street in Regina.

When I was nine, my parents adopted my Indigenous sister, Ruth, who was seven. We then moved to live in Winnipeg, and, in 1950 the Red River flooded and our basements and others in our neighbourhood had water and sewage back up. The Red Cross helped our neighbours financially with repairs to many furnaces. My Indigenous mother, my sister, and I waited in a long lineup. Without explanation, the Red Cross denied my mom's request for assistance, although all the others in the lineup were approved. Our white neighbours who needed assistance got help. Again, my parents did not bemoan the issue with Ruth or me.

My many other experiences of racism include the refusal of servers to wait on me in restaurants, not being helped by cashiers when I shop, and being asked many times by a close friend, "Are you Indian?" until I asked her if it made a difference to our friendship. She is still one of my closest friends.

In an unusual set of circumstances, when I was 17 and in my last year of high school, I met my future husband, Ed. This set me on a path of learning about the Indigenous way of life because even though Ed was not Indigenous, he had lived at the Frog Lake Reserve in east-central Alberta for 10 or so years. His non-Indigenous parents were school teachers for the children on the reserve, but were itinerant and taught in other places too, leaving Ed in the care of the Frog Lake community.

Not only did Ed become a fluent Cree speaker; he was also schooled in Cree ways. I had never heard Cree spoken before. My mother did not speak it. "Opposites attract," I've heard said, and this was so true in our situation. I was Indigenous, knew nothing about reserve life, and didn't speak Cree, and Ed was white, spoke the language, and was culturally more Indigenous than I would ever be. I recall now that Ed taught me how to say tawâw—welcome—when my parents welcomed him into our home soon after we met.

All the media attention paid to the Truth and Reconciliation Commission brought back a lot of bitter memories that I had worked hard to forget. I was not aware of the treaties or that I have lived in Treaty 4 territory, Treaty 1 territory, and Treaty 6 territory until my daughter Naomi and I discussed it recently. I now realize I must accept that the land my English-but-Canadian-born father inherited and farmed in Saskatchewan is Treaty 4 land, that Winnipeg and southern Manitoba are on Treaty 1 land, and that Edmonton, where I have lived since 1953, for seven decades, and owned property for six decades, is Treaty 6 land.

I must put aside and rationalize as only memories the hurts that I experienced as a child when excluded from play or the derision

I've experienced as an adult, such as when a friend's son was gifted with a few thousand dollars at his wedding and said, "Not bad for an Indian." Or when the aggressively racist couple at Smitty's restaurant who resisted sitting near me until told there were no other tables and then retaliated by reading loudly enough for everyone in the restaurant to hear articles in the *Edmonton Journal* about Indians breaking the law. Or when our family was refused service at a restaurant in the Citadel Theatre many years ago.

I choose instead to enjoy the lasting relationships of my nursing classmates, my nursing colleagues, my loving family, and the wonderful people in the Stroll of Poets with whom I've made treasured friendships, and, in hearing their beautiful readings, discovered my love for poetry.

Not Just a Land Acknowledgement

Naomi McIlwraith

Some First Nations people may opt out of doing land acknowledgements because they are on their own land and may feel that non-Indigenous peoples bear the responsibility of acknowledging Indigenous land. Nonetheless, many Indigenous peoples, when visiting the territories of other Indigenous peoples, will certainly express gratitude to the host nation or even a territorial acknowledgement. What do I do when I am both Indigenous and non-Indigenous?

First, I recognize my white privilege because, even though I own nothing but a canoe, a couple of bikes, a trusty, slightly rusty Ford Ranger, and too many books to count, I have what has been denied many Indigenous peoples: education, a home with a roof over my head, two parents who loved me, four grandparents who loved me, a job, and so much more.

It's important for me to state the many injustices imposed on Indigenous peoples throughout what we now call Canada. These include the Consolidated Indian Act, unfair treaties with broken promises by our first and all subsequent colonial governments, the horrors and traumas of Indian residential schools. Structural racism was central to an educational system that tried to "beat the Indian out of the child," punished children for speaking their mother tongues and for simply wanting to be Indigenous, and permitted the emotional, physical, and sexual abuse that Indigenous children suffered at those schools. Despite all this, my Indigenous hosts and neighbours generously allowed my non-Indigenous ancestors to settle here on Treaty 6 territory and, further back, on the territories of Treaties 1, 2, and 4.

I ask my Indigenous hosts to recognize that although my non-Indigenous paternal grandparents taught at the Edmonton Indian

Residential School here, it cuts me to the core to see the words "Possible Trigger" next to a picture of my grandfather, Charles McIlwraith, on an Edmonton Indian Residential School Facebook group. My grandfather tried to defend his Indigenous students by reporting what they reported to him, only to be removed from his position as a teacher and relocated to Alert Bay, a wee island off the northeast coast of Vancouver Island.

My life's work to figure out who I am as a white-skinned Métis woman includes listening to my mom's stories of her experiences with racism that began in kindergarten and continued through her life during her 37 years as a neonatal registered nurse. I wonder too what my nôhkom nitâniskotâpân (my great grandmother) Lillian and nôhkom (my grandmother) Lucabelle endured during their lifetimes.

My life's work also has me in the good company of those who, though not human, are just as sentient as we humans. So I feel compelled to acknowledge the many Indigenous peoples who inhabited Turtle Island before settlers came and who are still here: nêhiyawak, Anishinaabe, Ipiihkoohkanipiaohtsi, Dene, Métis, Nakota Isga Sioux, Karhiio (Mohawk), and Anirnik (Inuit), but I must also acknowledge the many birds, bugs, trees, rivers, pathways, stones, stars, mountains, lakes, grasslands, highlands, lowlands, and so many more who have imbued my life with meaning and enriched me beyond measure. In no way do I diminish my human hosts here by invoking those who are not human. I've learned that meaning on Earth is not the sole experience or property of humans. And it's a blessing to know that my relatives are both human and deeper-than-human.

In offering this humble land acknowledgement that isn't just a land acknowledgement, I commit to listening to Indigenous people's stories because they have been suppressed for far too long in Canada's colonial narrative. And I recommit to learning nêhiyawêwin, one of the languages of my maternal ancestors, the language that my wonderful father spoke even though he was not Indigenous.

In closing, I will say as many Indigenous peoples say in English, "All my relations," but I will say it in nêhiyawêwin, "kahkiyaw niwâhkômâkanak"; in Lakota, "Mitákuye Oyás'iŋ"; and in Anishinaabemowin, "Indinawemaaganidog."

My Humble Land Acknowledgement
to All Stewards of Treaty 6
ostêsimâwasinahikan nikotwâsik

Naomi McIlwraith

In the morning when Sun emerges
from his dreams, Eagle calls to us
from sâkâstênohk to tend the Fire
of this day's most glorious yellow beginning.

And we lean in to heed the teachings of kihêw.

Just before we take our noon meal,
Buffalo calls to us from sâwanohk
to tend the Earth of this day's most
resplendent crimson prairie.

And we lean in to heed the teachings of paskwâwi-mostos.

In the evening, Bear calls to us
from pahkisimotahk to tend the Water's
most pure and clear and blue and green
gifts that quench our hot dry thirst.

And we lean in to heed the teachings of maskwa.

At day's weary end, White Wolf calls to us
from kîwêtinohk, reminding us
to tend the very Air from where
we gather every blessed breath.

And we lean in to heed the teachings of wâpahihkan.

of Nakota Isga, Anirnik, tastawiyiniwak
of Dene, O-day'min, Métis, sipiwiyiniwak

of pâhpâstêw, pihêsiwin, Ipiihkoohkanipiaohtsi
of Karhiio, Sspomitapi
and of all those who tended and continue to tend
this magnificent land before us.

In offering this land acknowledgement, I pledge to continue my peacemaking work between Indigenous peoples and settlers.

With thanks to the Indigenous Knowledge Ward Naming Committee of Edmonton for assistance with the pronunciation of the Indigenous ward names in this poem.
ay hay! eesh neesh!
[A-NIR-NIK], [EE-PEEH-KOH-KA-NEEPIUH-TSI-YA],
[GAR-EE-HE-O], [SS-POH-ME-TAH-PEE]

The words have been all around

Don Perkins

The words have been all around and under us
            all these years,
in knowledge spoken
but unlistened-to outside
the circles of crushed truths;

Words denying acts
            squeezed out of the public record
            out of books, journals, official reports,
            and those other ledgers of infamy
hidden away for safe-keeping;

Words never carved into stones never erected
            over graves of the hidden dead,
or once carved and erected but long since
removed from sight and study.

In the words of the poet,
"…we live in a democracy erected
over the burial ground"[27] --
a burial ground no longer invisible
to technology or the re-emergent
public record, spoken and written.

The words are the names and the facts
            of the no-longer uncelebrated dead
            and of the less and less celebrated builders
            in the holy name of progress,
            of making something greater –

---

[27] Joy Harjo, "In Mystic," *Conflict Resolution for Holy Beings* (New York: Norton, 2015), 63.

uneasy partners in this something less
we have been making
in the mythical act of making it
true, strong, and free
out of someone else’s home
and native land.

When Crow Stole White Noise

Daniel Poitras

Edmonton is surrounded by 10 different First Nations reserves: Alexander, Alexis, Enoch, Ermineskin, Louis Bull, Michel, Montana, Paul, Saddle Lake, Samson.

Found one of their members down on her luck, on 101st Street and Jasper, leaned up against the Canadian Imperial Bank of Commerce building. I approached and asked if she was in danger? In need? In-digenous?

But she couldn't speak English. All that came out was sounds of water washing over rocks, pouring and pushing through stones and banks.

I dial 911 on my phone. "What's your emergency?"

I ask the woman, "What's wrong? How do you need help?" She makes sounds like hooves crunching onto leaves, like branches snapping against heavy bodies of fur. I nod solemnly. I tell the voice on the other end that she has been robbed.

"Sir, is she hurt or bleeding?"

She's been the victim of bloodletting for generations. She can't remember the prayer of her Grandfather, the smell of her Grandmother's cooking.

I follow her to the Chateau Lacombe, where she shows me tarps upon tarps, grocery carts filled with treasures I don't understand. She opens her mouth and crows chittering around a swamp, trying to croak like the frogs, come tumbling out.

"Hello! Are you still listening?"

"Yes, sir. I need a location to send . . ."

She's from Alexis, Louis Bull, Paul's, and Samson. She's still at the same place you sent her to die. Where the Elders smudge, sweat, and hold seances because the future keeps dying younger and younger. Still there where you sent the Indian agents, the Mounted Police, the Black Robes, where you sent death and despair to live.

She starts to rub her hands over and over and then locks them together, firm. Tears stream down her cheeks, running down the wrinkles and lines in her face. She begins to sob and chokes out rifle smoke, shells that sizzle in the dry grass, fire crackling to life to engulf the prairies and lick clean the bones of all the buffalo.

"Sir, is anyone in danger? Was there a robbery? Do I need to send the Poli- . . ."

Yes! YES! Send the police, the military, send body bags when help is requested. When we demonstrated peacefully and enjoyed—not occupied, enjoyed—our own lands you met that with assault rifles and riot shields. Pleaded for the stoppage of rape of Mother Earth for her resources, and you answered with land acknowledgements and street names.

She slumps to the ground, carefully, like a leaf crumpled and deteriorated. She holds a frail, withered arm across her belly. She brings the other withered hand, the one filled with invisible bannock, to her mouth. She chews on sounds that smell like campfire, like moose meat boiling in rice and raisins, like fried bologna bubbling up beside the sizzle of eggs.

"Sir! Sir! I . . ."

Want you to know she's terrified of your laws, your empty promises, your twisted words and gods. She's seen you tear away the babies from the arms of mothers. She's seen you season and cook them in your iron stoves. She has seen your Wendigos, wooden "T" dangling around their necks, granting them greed and clemency from their own laws. Granting hunger for little boys and girls. What are you going to offer this woman in danger, endangered, In-digenous?

A sigh answers. A long sigh that's meant to break the silence. A long sigh that's meant to cool the embers and ease the burns. A long sigh like white noise.

"Sir, I understand your frustration. For me to offer any help or solutions to address any of the needs of the woman in danger, I need . . ."

I cut them out of our life. I look down to the old woman.

"I'm sorry. They refuse to help. They only want to talk and talk. Good luck."

I leave, clench-fisted, to battle an indifferent world ahead of me.

A Gradual Awakening

Shirley Serviss

I grew up in Treaty 6, although I didn't know that then. I was aware that the land my father farmed had once been inhabited by Indigenous people. Arrowheads and stone hammer heads turned up in the fields and were collected by my brother.

I was made aware of residential schools one spring when two young boys were stranded in one of the fields by the runoff and rescued by my brother on his horse. They barely had time to warm up by the wood stove and finish the hot chocolate my mother made them before two nuns showed up looking for them. It didn't occur to me at the time to wonder what they were running from and that they left with the nuns.

Métis children went to the rural school with us. Métis men worked for our father and ate their meals with us. My beloved great aunt was Métis, born in a fort to an Indigenous woman and was married to my father's Irish uncle. It was not until I was an adult that I found out her ancestry was never discussed with her children and grandchildren, as though it was something to hide.

When I was 20, I spent a summer working on a housing project for non-status and Métis families in Kenora, living in the Indian Friendship Centre, clearing land with a machete and putting in foundations along with young people from all over the world. The hostility of white residents in the community opposed to the development came as a surprise to me. We were called names as we rode to the job site in the back of a truck, and people refused to let their teens have anything to do with us. On a weekend camping trip to Winnipeg, after being denied admission to places where we wanted to have a beer and dance, I found out what a city looks like from the sidewalk.

It took conversations with Indigenous people about the abuse they suffered, including a patient who told me about having to dig the graves for the younger children, before I learned what went on at residential schools. At the hearings of the Truth and Reconciliation Commission, I listened to the testimonies with silent tears running down my cheeks. The Indigenous woman sitting beside me reached out and took my hand. It was a powerful moment for me, but I felt undeserving. I should have been the one consoling her.

I knew treaties existed but wrongly assumed these applied only to the Indigenous people. I didn't realize the treaties made us kin and applied equally to the settlers, their descendants, and the immigrants who came afterwards. The signing of the treaties meant we were equals and would recognize and honour the belief systems, way of life, and governance systems of the First Nations.

To me, land acknowledgements are an important opportunity to remember that the treaties were based on friendship, peace and respect and that we are honour bound to live up to those commitments.

The Ground Remembers: A Treaty 6 Territory Acknowledgement

patti sinclair

I thank the people of the Papaschase nation and the sacred land of Treaty 6 territory where the Papaschase people gathered, fished, and shared in ceremony.

"The ground remembers, and occasionally still floods in times of heavy rains,"[28] Matthew James Weigel says in his book, *Whitemud Walking.*

For 25 of the past 30 years I have lived on lakes. I did not know this until my house flooded in 2004. The dark deluge quietly and methodically invaded, shocked, and infected our home. Our exhaustion was deep and wide. We learned our house was built on top of McKernan Lake, which was drained in order to develop more homesteads. We had insurance. Everything was wrapped up within three months.

It is 2023. I have now lived in Edmonton's Parkallen neighbourhood for the last dozen years. It too, was once a drained lake. Reading Weigel's book, a dam broke inside me. I learn these lakes were places where Indigenous peoples once gathered, fished, and shared ceremony.

These peoples were part of the Papaschase reserve. Their reserve was taken through fraud. Settlers squatted on these lands. The true dark deluge quietly and methodically invaded, shocked, and infected their traditional lands. Their gathering places were taken away.

---

[28] Matthew James Weigel, "Edmonton City Planning: 1890-2022," *Whitemud Walking* (Toronto: Coach House Books, 2022), 100.

I thought I knew the Indigenous history of Treaty 6 territory. Only this year I more deeply recognize the lands I have lived on for 25 years were taken from the Papaschase people.[29]

In 2022, Parkallen was part of a $55 million flood mitigation project. Two dry ponds were built to act as catch basins for excess stormwater during heavy rainfalls. A community garden was also completed, with three benches.

The Papaschase nation no longer owns the land they negotiated under Treaty 6. They were expelled from their own land. The last of them left on August 12, 1887.

I thank the people of the Papaschase nation of Treaty 6 territory where the Papaschase people gathered, fished, and shared ceremony. The numbered treaties were based on the Indigenous perspective of sharing.[30] These lands have held, birthed, and healed my settler family. With deep gratitude to the ground for remembering.

---

[29] https://www.epl.ca/blogs/post/yeg-wards-discover-yourneighbourhood/#ward8:
"When land was surveyed for the Papaschase Band in 1880 south of the North Saskatchewan River, they were given a 40-square-mile plot, too small to meet the needs of their 249 members. The local Indian Agent then arbitrarily transferred people off the band list. Additionally, local settlers didn't want the community too close and petitioned the federal government to eventually force the band into complete surrender. Facing starvation, the breakup of their community, and pressure from local settlers, a small number of the remaining members eventually surrendered their land. Surviving members of the Papaschase Band are working to reclaim their community and land in the area."

[30] "The numbered treaties were based on the Indigenous perspective of sharing." (Naomi McIlwraith, personal communication, March 16, 2023).

Healing and Hope

Laurel Sproule

Tansi, (Cree) Taansi (Métis)

Welcome to amiskwaciy-wâskahikan.

The Stroll of Poets acknowledges that we meet on Treaty 6 territory, a traditional land of Plains Cree, Anishinaabe, Sioux or Assiniboine, Dene, Blackfoot, and Métis peoples. The land we meet on is still Indigenous land.

Reconciliation is desired by Stroll members, which involves learning what occurred when Indigenous people met with representatives of the Crown of England and the Government of Canada, who imposed treaties on them that the Crown used to justify taking the land Indigenous peoples had occupied for centuries.

Treaties were unilateral impositions. So-called negotiations were conducted in English, without translation for Indigenous peoples. Crown representatives ignored the needs and traditions of Indigenous peoples in favour of speedy resolutions.

When the land was stolen from Indigenous people, they were promised things never delivered. Understanding the history between Canada and Indigenous people isn't enough, but it is a necessary first step to reconciliation, according to Stephen Marche, resident of Ontario and author of "Canada's Impossible Acknowledgment" in The *New Yorker*, September 7, 2017.

In Edmonton, on Treaty 6 land, a traditional territory, we benefit from Indigenous peoples' stewardship of the land and the waterways of the North Saskatchewan River. We acknowledge the unextinguished Indigenous rights to the land where we meet to read poetry. We are thankful to meet here.

We unite in equity and understanding, committed to fostering relationships to overcome the impact of colonization and the injustices of the treaties.

hiy hiy

Thank you.

Thank You for Honouring the Earth

Max Vandersteen

I came to Canada at a young age and consider myself an Albertan now, since I grew up in Calgary and Edmonton and have now resided in Edmonton for almost 50 years. I have enjoyed numerous activities in the outdoor wilderness of Treaty 6 and Treaty 7 land in this province, including camping, hiking, fishing, skiing, and horseback riding.

Always it was a thrill to enjoy nature, breathe the air, and soak up the sun and the sights in the mountains, lakes, or back woods. I was fortunate to have worked in the once pristine lands of Treaty 8 instead of in the dense population of the city for a portion of my career.

I would like to acknowledge those who lived here before me for preserving these lands and wondrous sights, in particular the Indigenous people who dwelled in this area for generations. As I see it, we have to continue their culture of recognizing the beauty that the Creator has bestowed on us, the importance of revering it, and the necessity of maintaining its integrity for others after us.

I am dismayed at some of the present treatment of our resources and abuses of the land that are occurring. We must learn to practice control, conservation, and respect in order that our grandchildren and First Nations grandchildren can still enjoy the outdoor activities that I enjoyed while growing up in this province.

Contributor Biographies

Stefani Alzati is a writer, visual artist, and teacher from Ottawa, Ontario. She grew up camping, foraging, and creating deep connections with the land in and around amiskwaciy-wâskahikan. She embraces mindfulness and somatics in her poetry to release poems from where they live in the bones and muscles of the body. You can find her poetry on Instagram @Stefani.Alzati.

Hank Binnema is a poet who has lived on Treaty 6 territory for most of his adult life. He lives in amiskwaciy-wâskahikan, ward Métis. He's still learning what it means to be an immigrant in a land amidst beautiful Indigenous nations. He is grateful to Amitav Ghosh's moving account in *The Nutmeg's Curse: Parables for a Planet in Crisis* (Chicago: Chicago University Press, 2021) of the Banda Islands massacre, a part of Hank's history he was unfamiliar with until he was in his 60s.

Audrey Brooks was born in 1940, in a Carragana, Saskatchewan, nursing station, in Treaty 4 territory and now resides in the sipiwiyiniwak ward. Since 1987 she has lived in amiskwaciy-wâskahikan, part of Treaty 6 territory known as Edmonton. A retired Unitarian chaplain, Audrey's service includes 10 years with the U of Alberta Interfaith Chaplains Association, chaplain with the Truth and Reconciliation Commission, spiritual counsellor with Camp Fyrefly at the University of Alberta, four years on the Academic Senate of St. Stephen's College at the University of Alberta, long-term Raging Granny, and host for Ukrainian refugees.

David C. Brydges is a cultural entrepreneur and community legacy builder in Cobalt, Ontario. He is the artistic director of the Spring Pulse Poetry Festival in Northern Ontario. Memberships include the Stroll of Poets, Parkland Poets, Ontario Poetry Society, Haiku Canada, and League of Canadian

Poets. In 2021 he was appointed the first Poet Emissary for the Ontario Poetry Society, replacing a yearly recognition of the Poet of the Year. David has published six chapbooks, including his latest, *Vaulting to Venus,* and one full-length book, *Vagabond Post Office.*

Kayleigh Cline (she/her) has been most recently published in *FreeFall, Prairie Fire,* and *CV2.* Her work has also appeared on a bus and on a beer. Her poem “American Robin” won the Alberta Magazine Award for Poetry in 2022. An active member of the Stroll of Poets Society and the Canty Collective of Writerly Women, she was born in Mohkínstsisi and lives in Edmonton, Alberta, amiskwaciy-wâskahikan, ward pâhpâstêw.

Leslie Y. Dawson is a retired newspaper writer and editor, a reporter, a magazine writer, and an environmental and medical writer and editor. She has published countless articles, three nonfiction books, and a poetry book. She is now working on a second true crime book, a young adult novel, and helped produce this book. Currently she serves on the board of the Stroll of Poets Society. She was born on unceded land in Toronto, Ontario, and now lives in the Métis ward of Edmonton, on Treaty 6 land.

Dr. Deidra Suwanee Dees was born on the Indigenous land of Mvskoke, her ancestors’ land, and she still lives on the same land on which she was born, land the settlers named Alabama.

Janis Dow Durnin was born in Winnipeg and raised in Killarney, Manitoba on Treaty 1 Territory. She now resides in Treaty 6 Territory, in ward Métis, in Edmonton. Janis has been involved with the Stroll of Poets Society since 2016 and served as vice president and president. In the fall of 2021, after feeling the devastation of the finding of the remains of 215 Indigenous children on the grounds of residential schools in Kamloops, B.C., she helped to bring more personal and meaningful land acknowledgements to the Stroll of Poets and Unity of

Edmonton. This book project is close to Janis's heart because she is an adoptee through the closed adoption system in Canada. Through her own reconciliation with her family of origin she can relate, in part, to the trauma felt by those who have been taken from their families of origin and culture and raised by others, such as the injustices experienced by residential school victims, survivors, and their families and by people affected by the 60s Scoop.

Douglas Elves in 2019 published the book *Riverlines, Poems of Time and Place along the North Saskatchewan River.* In university he studied classics, literature, and languages. His experience in many community and arts organizations and in the labour movement enabled him to convene the founding committee of the Edmonton Stroll of Poets Society, a democratic society in which he served as treasurer for many years. His website is http://www.riverlines.ca Douglas was born in Edmonton. The civic ward he lives in he calls niso, which is Cree for ward 2. He does not accept what he calls the obfuscating names recently given to Edmonton's previously numbered wards. The intention of such a move, he says, was clearly to disenfranchise a large segment of the population, who would find the names so hard to pronounce and remember that they would throw up their hands and choose to disengage from voting procedures. The opposite of inclusive. He says we can still honour the Cree heritage by adopting simpler names: ward piyak, ward niso, ward nisto, etc. for wards 1, 2, 3, and so on. Everyone uses numbers. Instead of turning voters away, he says, we can charm them with the chance to learn the simple Cree sequence of numbers.

Lynn Gale (she, her, hers) is a poet and writer living within Treaty 6 territory near asinîskâwi-maskotêw (Stony Plain). She seeks stillness in her life to better hear the messages in the pauses and understand the truth hidden in the past.

Gary Garrison was born in Muskogee, Oklahoma, the U.S. state originally known as Indian Territory, where, in the 19th century, over 60 tribes from elsewhere were forcibly relocated. Gary's mother said that he and his three siblings could have claimed treaty rights because their paternal grandmother was Cherokee, but that would have required formally recognizing their ancestry at a time and in a place where the Ku Klux Klan thrived and Indigenous people ranked below even blacks in the social hierarchy. He currently lives in ward pâhpâstêw in Edmonton, part of the Beaver Hills area Cree people named amiskwaciy-wâskahikan.

Trudy Grienauer is a storyteller and student of life from Edmonton, Alberta. She has published in *The Fieldstone Review* and *The Prairie Journal* and is a regular contributor to Edmonton's Stroll of Poets. Two of her poems have been included in the hardcover anthology *Vistas of the West*. Her poem "Rossdale, April" travelled on Edmonton buses as part of the Edmonton Transit System (ETS) Poetry Route, and her song, "To Walk in Beauty," in honor of missing and murdered Indigenous women, was performed by the Edmonton Metropolitan Chorus. She was born in Bavaria and now lives in amiskwaciy-wâskahikan, on Treaty 6 lands, in ward pâhpâstêw.

Lois Mary Hammond was born in Treaty 6 territory (amiskwaciy-wâskahikan/Edmonton) and lives there in ward sipiwiyiniwak. She reads and writes poetry because it's one portal into life beyond the surfaces. She was privileged to work briefly with Ralph Steinhauer, honoured Indigenous leader and Alberta's 10th Lieutenant-Governor, and to tutor Huu-ay-aht children from Anacala, B.C. They taught her much.

Trevor Hughes' first live encounter with poetry was with the Mersey Poets, Brian Patten, Roger McGough, and Adrian Henri in the 60's in his native Liverpool. He has been hooked ever since. His sequence of poems, *Belongings,* was published by

Kingston Press, Hull, in 2017. After a career as an English teacher, he spent several years living in Normandy and then Alsace before moving to Edmonton.

Melle Huizinga was a long-time member of the Stroll of Poets. He died in January 2019. Melle had a lifelong thirst for justice. He was an addiction counselor with the Nechi Centre, which supports Indigenous culture and spiritual practices to promote healing and wellness. He volunteered at Truth and Reconciliation events, and he initiated and facilitated a First Nations, Métis, and Inuit module offered by The King's University to its education students. His widow, Dolores, has graciously offered Melle's poem for inclusion here. It originally appeared in the Stroll's 2015 anthology. Their home is in Edmonton's ward O-day'min.

Dan Knauss was born in Poughkeepsie, New York, which is an English-ed name for Uppuqui-ipis-ing, meaning "the reed-covered lodge by the little water place" in the Eastern Algonquian Munsee language of the Wappinger tribe located there when the Dutch and English arrived. The etymological origin of "Wappinger" is unknown and has many spelling variants. It could be a corruption of a negative Dutch term, "weapon draggers," or a Munsee word for opossum.

Josephine LoRe, *"a pearl in this diamond world,"* has shared her work live and in global Zoom-rooms. Her words have been put to music, danced, interpreted in ASL, and integrated into visual art. She has two collections, *Unity* and the *Calgary Herald* bestseller *The Cowichan Series,* and has been published in literary magazines and anthologies in 15 countries and five languages. Her poem "Enough" was selected for a Feed the Children PSA in the US. Josephine respectfully acknowledges that she lives and creates on the ancestral and traditional lands of the Piikani, Siksika, Kainai, Tsuut'ina, Nakota, and Dene peoples. https://www.josephinelorepoet.com/

Dorothy Lowrie was born and still lives in Treaty 6 territory. Her home is in St. Albert, an area First Nations people call Payhonin, “gathering place.” She has loved and collected poetry all her life. She is blessed with an inheritance of the love of words in story, poetry, and music. In the new chapter of her life that has given her back the gift of time, she enjoys reflecting on her life and the world through learning and practicing the art of poetry.

Alice Major is a founding member of the Stroll of Poets and served as the City of Edmonton’s first poet laureate. She has published 12 collections of poetry and received multiple awards for her work, most recently the Lieutenant Governor of Alberta Distinguished Artist Award and an honorary doctorate from the University of Alberta. She grew up in Scarborough, Ontario, the traditional territory of many nations, including the Mississaugas of the Credit, the Anishnabeg, the Chippewa, the Haudenosaunee, and the Wendat peoples. She now lives in amiskwaciy-wâskahikan, now called Edmonton, in ward O-day’min.

Lavona McIlwraith was born in Lestock, Saskatchewan, a small town in Treaty 4 territory, and moved to Regina when she was five. When she was nine, Lavona, her new sister, Ruth, and her mom and dad moved to Treaty 1 territory to live in Winnipeg for five years. Then they moved west to Edmonton where Lavona has lived in Treaty 6 territory for seven decades. She worked for 37 years as a neonatal intensive care unit nurse at the Royal Alexandra Hospital, where all four of her children were born. Lavona and her husband Mowat (Ed) also served for many years as foster parents to wee babies needing a safe home. Their foster home, contrary to popular belief, was not a residential school but a safe loving home. She lived in Edmonton’s ward Nakota Isga until her death in early 2024.

Naomi McIlwraith hails from ward Nakota Isga in amiskwacî-wâskahikan, Plains Cree for Beaver Hills House, also known as Edmonton. In all that she does, Naomi honours her parents, Lavona and Mowat McIlwraith, her four grandparents, Lucabelle and James Meakes and Davida and Charles McIlwraith. As a Cree-Ojibwe-Métis writer, Naomi is grateful for her education and pledges to use it to build a more peaceful world. Born and raised here, she has wandered near and far, but always manages to find her way back to her home on Treaty 6 land. A teacher, a talker, a poet, and a peacemaker, she now works as an Indigenous interpreter, supervisor, researcher, and writer at the new Indigenous People's Experience at Fort Edmonton Park, over there by that wee bend in the North Saskatchewan River, just upstream of that bridge some call the Quesnell.

Aaron Paquette is a city councillor and a lifelong Edmontonian. He lives in ward Dene with his wife Clarice and their four children. Prior to his election, Aaron worked as an award-winning Indigenous artist and author. His work can be viewed in museums, schools, hospitals and LRT stations throughout Edmonton. His novel, *Lightfinder*, is taught in schools and post-secondary institutions across Canada. He has also worked with local schools in Edmonton's north side to help create mural projects. His passion for education also led him to work with Alberta Education, various school boards and teachers' associations to help develop art curriculum and improve academic achievement. In 2012, he created an education conference to lay new ground for more effective approaches to creating healthy and respectful learning environments for students and teachers.

Don Perkins was born in Victoria, B.C., on the lands of the Esquimalt Nation. He writes now from Edmonton, (amiskwaciy-wâskahikan) ward pâhpâstêw, in Treaty 6 territory where he taught at the University of Alberta, including courses in Native and Aboriginal literature for the Department of English and Film Studies, as well as introductory courses for the Faculty of Native Studies and for Native Student Services.

Daniel Poitras is a half-breed poet from the Paul First Nation in Treaty 6 territory. Currently residing in Stony Plain, he writes about the challenges that Indigenous and Métis people face today. He has been published in the *Home and Away* anthology (House of Blue Skies, 2009), *The Malahat Review*, *Grain Magazine*, *The Polyglot,* and in the Edmonton Poetry Festival's Poetry Moves on Transit program.

Shirley A. Serviss lives in ward O-day'min of Edmonton (amiskwaciy-wâskahikan) within Treaty 6 territory and the Métis Nation of Alberta Region 4. She has published three poetry collections and co-edited two anthologies. Her poetry and essays have appeared in numerous magazines and collections. A long-time member of the writing community, she has served on numerous arts boards and juries and volunteered at literary festivals. Shirley has mentored many local writers as a publisher, editor, teacher, and writer-in-residence.

patti sinclair was born, lives, and creates in Treaty 6 territory on the sacred land of the Papaschase. Her writing includes *THE RIGHTFUL SKIN,* launched with London's *Rose Garden Press*, a collection of poems on origins, patterns of suffering, and searching for home and truth between layers of earth and skin. patti's forthcoming, *the late season,* a long poem, is to be published with Winnipeg's, At Bay Press. For more about patti see @locating the beauty on Instagram and poet-at-large.blogspirit.com.

Laurel Sproule was born and lived on Treaty 1 territory in Winnipeg, the traditional lands of Anishinaabe, Cree, Dene, and Dakota. It is also the birthplace of Louis Riel and the Métis Nation. She lived in Quebec and England before returning to

Canada for university. After a career in education, she writes poetry, fiction, and non-fiction. Her poetry received a James Patrick Folinsbee Scholarship from the University of Alberta, and a screenplay, *Lift*, was a 2016 finalist in the AMPIA awards. She's revising a novella, *No Way Out but Through;* a YA novel, *Whale;* and a novel, *High Definition*, and completing a short story collection, *In the Neighbourhood*. She lives on Treaty 6 territory in ward Métis, the name gifted to the City of Edmonton for municipal elections. Ward Métis is near the North Saskatchewan River, where Métis people settled and farmed.

Max Vandersteen was born in Wycheproof (derived from the Aborigine word witchi-poorp, which means grass on a hill), Australia, moved to Canada at a young age and grew up in Alberta. He presently lives in ward Dene in the city of Edmonton (amiskwaciy-wâskahikan). He is a retired pipefitter who resumed writing poetry after a career in the petrochemical industry. Max strives to use poetry to express concerns regarding social justice issues, including reconciliation, environmental consequences of our resource and land use, and the need to deal with these concerns.

Thank You

nêhiyawêwin – Plains Cree – is not the only Indigenous language in the Edmonton area, but it provides insight into what acknowledging means in the context of reconciliation. One way to say "acknowledgement" in nêhiyawêwin is with the noun naskwêwasihtwâwin. The verb naskwêwasim means "to answer," and the verb naskwê-osih means "to repair something along the way." Acknowledge. Answer. Repair.

This book takes a tentative step to acknowledge, answer, and repair our relationships with Indigenous peoples. We thank the many Stroll of Poets members who are committed to good relations with Indigenous peoples and have shared their efforts and experiences in this work, especially those who submitted contributions to this book.

Making this anthology involved a small group of people, to whom we extend our gratitude for their belief in this project and for their support. The Land Acknowledgement Committee thanks the many Indigenous peoples who welcomed or put up with settlers for centuries and tolerated meaningless land acknowledgements in recent years. We hope the statements in this collection are an improvement. We ask you to be patient as we decolonize our minds.

We are grateful to Councillor Aaron Paquette for endorsing this collection with his Foreword. Cree Elder Kathy Hamelin and her daughter Remy Boudreau (they/them) reviewed the manuscript and offered an Indigenous perspective on how to improve it. Thank you very much, Kathy and Remy! Thank you to Randal Kabatoff and Circle Teachings for introducing us to Kathy and Remy and for being part of the review process.

To the Stroll of Poets Board of Directors, we offer deep gratitude for your support, moral, conceptual, and financial, which has been critical to this collection's becoming a reality.

We also thank Don Perkins and Sara Coumantarakis, our proofreaders, and the Stroll's Administrative Assistant, Christyn Carter, as well as the Writers' Guild of Alberta, the Edmonton Arts Council, and the Alberta Foundation for the Arts. This book is one of the Stroll's numerous initiatives that these agencies have supported for many years.

And to you, dear reader, we offer our thanks for choosing to read this book, for beginning your own work of facing and healing Canada's mistakes, and for working with us for a fairer, more equal, anti-racist Canada.

This book did not happen overnight, and neither will decolonizing our minds. Acknowledge. Answer. Repair. This is a beginning.

Land Acknowledgments Project Committee
Leslie Y. Dawson, Janis Dow Durnin, Gary Garrison,
Naomi McIlwraith

Editor's Notes

Style Decisions Regarding Indigenous Words

The committee responsible for this book wrestled with how to style Indigenous words and phrases. First, should we italicize them or not? Opaskwayak Cree editor Gregory Younging and other Indigenous editors present a compelling argument in favour of not italicizing Indigenous words because we need to normalize rather than exoticize Indigenous words and languages.[31] This is an exciting deviation from the standard practice of italicizing non-English words in an English-language publication!

Second, what capitalization style suits these words and phrases? In Plains Cree, which is the most common Indigenous language in Treaty 6 territory where we live, the practice is always to lowercase them, even if they are proper names of people or places and even if they begin a sentence. Further, Plains Cree has more firmly established rules for orthography than other Indigenous languages in the Canadian west. So, we decided to use lowercase letters for all Cree words and phrases, except for those we know are not in Plains Cree.

We have one person on the committee who has expertise in Plains Cree but not in other Indigenous languages. For words outside her expertise, we decided to follow the example of the Indigenous Ward Naming Knowledge Committee of the city of Edmonton. As a concrete act of reconciliation, city council asked this group of Indigenous matriarchs to recommend names for the previously numbered 12 civic wards in Edmonton. In December 2020, Edmonton City Council adopted the Indigenous names

[31] Gregory Younging, *Elements of Indigenous Style: A Guide for Writing By and About Indigenous Peoples* (Edmonton: Brush Education Inc., 2018).

those matriarchs submitted. The list of ward names, their meanings and pronunciations are available at

https://www.edmonton.ca/city government/city_organization/indigenous-ward-naming-knowledge-committee

Our committee decided, wherever possible, to use the spellings and capitalization styles of those ward names, and we have asked all the poets who have pieces in this book to note in their biographies the Indigenous names of the wards where they live. Biographies of poets who live outside Edmonton include Indigenous place names for their place of residence, wherever possible.

A Caveat on Terminology

Words hurt and words heal, so as we work to repair broken relationships between the Canadian settler state and Indigenous peoples, we also need to educate ourselves on the changing connotations and senses of the words we use. We offer this list to help you understand why some words seemed okay in times past but are now worse than out-of-date.

Indian—We hesitate but are compelled sometimes to use the word "Indian" because it is inaccurate and brutally hurtful, but it is part of our history and is enshrined in law. We have in Canada the Consolidated Indian Act, we have "Indian Residential Schools," and countless Indigenous people in our nation experience daily the trauma of this word flung viciously at them.

Aboriginal—Although a part of our Constitution and a legal term in Canada, this word has lost its shine. It legally acknowledges First Nations, Métis, and Inuit peoples as Aboriginal. Many of these peoples find it woefully inadequate.

First Nations—Because First Nations hold reserve lands and are entitled to treaty rights, they are distinct from Métis and Inuit peoples. As a term, "First Nations" was first used in 1980 when hundreds of chiefs met in Ottawa to deliver their Declaration of First Nations and to provide a different term to use than "Indian." Their legal rights are under federal jurisdiction.

Métis—People of mixed Indigenous and European descent, Métis peoples constantly wrestle with the political and cultural complexities surrounding the term. Political organization has helped the Métis gain recognition as Aboriginal peoples in Canada with certain but limited rights within the Constitution and Supreme Court decisions. Métis peoples are subject to provincial laws.

Inuit—Indigenous people of Canada who have historically inhabited the northern regions of the Arctic. The Inuit homeland is known as Inuit Nunagat, which means the land, water, and ice across the Arctic region. The Inuit do not enjoy the same rights as First Nations people, though both groups are subject to federal laws and have experienced the harms of colonization along with First Nations and Métis peoples.

Indigenous—Following the United Nations Declaration on the Rights of Indigenous People (UNDRIP) in Brazil on 13 September, 2007, the word "Indigenous" has entered our lexicon. At first, Canada, the United States, England, and New Zealand, voted against UNDRIP. After Canada's Truth and Reconciliation Commission, the government endorsed UNDRIP, and since then, the word "Indigenous" has gained favour here. Though "Indigenous" is not a legal term in Canada in the way that "Aboriginal" is, "Indigenous" has powerful connotations that "Aboriginal" lacks. "Indigenous" provides opportunity for Indigenous peoples around the world to find solidarity with each other, as they work to reclaim what was stolen from them throughout their history and in their relationships with colonizers.

Reconciliation—Since the Truth and Reconciliation Commission of Canada finished its final report in 2015, we hear "Reconciliation" frequently in conversations across the country. Reconciliation is a necessary process because of the ongoing traumas of Indian Residential Schools and other injustices that Indigenous peoples experience. Many Indigenous peoples recognize that lip service too often passes as reconciliation, but for non-Indigenous people, genuine reconciliation means to educate themselves on Indigenous history and ongoing injustice and to set things right. This book attempts to do just that.

Treaty—The numbered treaties (1-11) are legal agreements between First Nations and the Canadian government made between 1871 and 1921. They took enormous tracts of land from Indigenous peoples. Extending from central Ontario to central British Columbia and the Northwest Territories, this treaty land was never "ceded" to Canada. Nevertheless, Canadian governments opened it for settlers, agriculture, towns, cities, highways, pipelines, resource extraction plants, and other uses. First Nations peoples interpret the treaties as sacred covenants between sovereign nations that extend through history to the current time, but Canadian governments past and present have often failed to honour the substance of these treaties, much less their longevity and sacredness.

The websites below map the extent of each treaty's territory, including the unnumbered treaties negotiated in eastern Canada, and identify the dates of each treaty.

Historical Treaty Boundaries in Canada

https://www.otc.ca/ckfinder/userfiles/files/Canada%20Treaty%20Boundaries.pdf

https://s3.amazonaws.com/libapps/accounts/5996/images/map_-_treaties2.jpg

https://www.rcaanc-cirnac.gc.ca/DAM/DAM-CIRNAC-RCAANC/DAM-TAG/STAGING/images-images/al_treaties_history_mapimage_1370362052588_eng.jpg

https://mediaindigena.com/wp-content/uploads/2013/01/treaties.png

https://www.canadashistory.ca/explore/settlement-immigration/the-numbered-treaties

Suggestions for Further Reading

Cardinal, Harold and Walter Hildebrandt. *Treaty Elders of Saskatchewan: Our Dream is That Our Peoples Will One Day Be Clearly Recognized as Nations.* Calgary: University of Calgary Press, 2000.

Craft, Aimée. *Treaty Words: For as Long as the Rivers Flow*. Toronto: Annick Press, 2021.

Joseph, Bob. *21 Things You May Not Know About the Indian Act: Helping Canadians Make Reconciliation with Indigenous Peoples a Reality*. Port Coquitlam, British Columbia: Indigenous Relations Press, 2018.

King, Thomas. *The Inconvenient Indian: A Curious Account of Native People in North America.* Toronto: Anchor Canada, 2013.

Mann, Charles. *1491: New Revelations of the Americas before Columbus*. New York: Random House, 2006.

Manuel, Albert. *The Reconciliation Manifesto: Recovering the Land, Rebuilding the Economy*. Toronto: James Lorimer & Company Ltd., 2013.

McDonald, John Brady. *Carrying it Forward: Essays from Kistahpinânihk.* Hamilton: Wolsak & Wynn, 2022.

Price, Richard T. *Legacy: Indian Treaty Relationships.* Edmonton: Plains Publishing Inc., 1991.

Teillet, Jean. *The North-West Is Our Mother: The Story of Louis Riel's People, the Métis Nation.* Toronto: Harper Collins Canada, 2019.

The Métis Association of Alberta and Joe Sawchuk, Patricia Sawchuk, and Theresa Ferguson. *Métis Land Rights in Alberta: A Political History*. Edmonton, Alberta: Métis Association of Alberta, 1981.

United Nations. *United Nations Declaration on the Rights of Indigenous Peoples*.
https://www.un.org/development/desa/indigenouspeoples/wp-content/uploads/sites/19/2018/11/UNDRIP_E_web.pdf
https://social.desa.un.org/issues/indigenous-peoples/united-nations-declaration-on-the-rights-of-indigenous-peoples

Vowel, Chelsea. *Indigenous Writes: A Guide to First Nations, Métis & Inuit Issues in Canada*. Winnipeg: Highwater Press, 2016.

Internet Resources

Cindy Blackstock, First Nations Family and Caring Society https://fncaringsociety.com/

ICT News, a Division of IndiJ Public Media. "Is It Time to Move Beyond Land Acknowledgements? Native non-profit leaders call for making reparations to tribes and returning tribal homelands"
https://ictnews.org/news/is-it-time-to-move-beyond-land-acknowledgements?eType=EmailBlastContent&eId=9d18bc61-71c1-4308-bf39-25f293c3e6e0

David A. Robertson, "Talking to Children and Youth about Residential Schools"
https://kplkids.wordpress.com/2021/06/15/david-a-robertson-talking-to-children-and-youth-about-residential-schools/

Upstander Project: Doctrine of Discovery
https://upstanderproject.org/learn/guides-and-resources/first-light/doctrine-of-discovery

Search suggestions

Explore online searches using the following phrases. The results will offer you many ways to connect and make contributions to Indigenous communities where you live.

- Indigenous-owned businesses
- Indigenous artists
- Indigenous crafts
- Indigenous stores near me
- Indigenous organizations
- Indigenous scholarships
- Indspire
- First Nations businesses

- Shop First Nations
- Native Canadian gifts
- Native owned-Etsy Canada
- Indigenous tourism near me
- Indigenous tourism Alberta
- Indigenous charities near me
- Indigenous charities in Canada
- Métis businesses

Indigenous Words for Buffalo/Bison

Some would argue that the great beasts of the North American plains are bison and that we can only find buffalo in Africa (cape buffalo) or Asia (water buffalo). Like many Indigenous peoples, non-Indigenous Canadians tend to use the words bison and buffalo interchangeably. Listed below are a variety of names Indigenous groups in the northern plains call this important animal.

nêhiyawêwin (Plains Cree language): paskwâwi-mostoswak
Niitsitapi (Siksika, Blackfoot Confederacy): iinii
Stoney (Stoney Nakoda Sioux): pté (female) and tatânka
(tȟatȟáŋka*)* (male)
Tsuut'ina Gunaha (Dene peoples west of Calgary): Xānı́-tı́ı́
Dene (Athapaskan peoples): nı̨nteliı̨jeré
Anishinaabemowin (Ojibwe peoples): Maskode-bishiki
Arapaho (Indigenous peoples, Plains of Colorado and
Wyoming): bii (female) or henéécee (male)
Salish (Indigenous peoples of the Pacific northwest): qweqway
Ani'-Yun'wiya' (Cherokee peoples): ya-na-sa